Starting Over & Loving It

By

Lakita D. Long

©2013 Lakita D. Long
All rights reserved. No portion of this book may be reproduced, stored in a retrieval system, or transmitted in any form or by any means-electronic, mechanical, photocopy, recording, scanning, or other-except for brief quotations in critical reviews or articles, without the prior written permission of the publisher.

Published in Antioch, California by Inspiring You Press.

All scripture quotations unless otherwise marked are taken from the King James Version

Cover Design: Gina Dacus of FUN Principle, www.funprinciple.com

Long, Lakita
 Starting Over and Loving It/ by Lakita Long

ISBN: 978-0-9790660-6-1

Copyright © 2013 Lakita D. Long
All rights reserved.
ISBN-13: 978-0-9790660-6-1

DEDICATION

I dedicate this book to every woman and man, who has had to start over in any aspect of their life, albeit career, family, lifestyle, spiritually, and mentally, and really did not like the process. Actually it felt like it was a cruel trick or bad nightmare happening in your life, and you just wanted it to end for a long enough period of time so that you could breathe.

I also dedicate this to the people who made it difficult for others to Start Over and Love It and I pray that you find complete peace in your life, knowing that you probably really didn't know what it was that you were doing in the first place. I pray that you would have the conscience of mind, if you dare and go back to the person that you may have caused unjust harm.

For every struggle, every place that remained not well, I pray that as you read this book, your life and heart is filled with joy and peace and the comfort of knowing that this too will pass.

May you all come to understand that the price that one pays for something is the complete liberty for others, such was demonstrated in Christ's dying that those who might believe would have life, and that more abundantly.

Even the price that you have had to pay for your pain and suffering, it was designed to liberate someone else, and it will as you purposefully re-language your story hit the hearts and ears of those that are waiting to live again.

May you see purpose in your life even after the storm, and you may never forget to tell your story, as it is a form of paying it forward.

CONTENTS

Acknowledgments
Preface
Introduction

SECTION ONE- The Backdrop

1. The Backdrop: A Brief Look At The Beginning
2. Growing Weary, Staying In Place
3. The Argument and the Accident Before the Wedding
4. The Wedding and Being At Home
5. Ignoring The REAL Truth, Living The Lie

SECTION TWO-*Living To Tell, Dying To Live*

6. The Courage to Leave
7. Despondent, Discouraged and Depressed
8. The Reality of Divorce and Separation From Anything
9. I Don't Love This

SECTION THREE-*Starting Over, Letting Go & Loving It*
"Strength From Within: The Power To Start Again"

10. The Mental Climb Back
11. Stress, Physical Fatigue and Sickness
12. Spiritual Momentum
    -Regaining Self-Respect
13. Gaining Godly Contentment
    -Loving The Skin Your In
14. The Journey is the Risk and the Reward

BONUS Chapters and Writings: To Inspire and Encourage

15. The Best Way To Help Others
16. When Life Gets Clogged UP The Desire For ORder
17. Upgrade Your Worth
18. The Peace Within: A Chat To Women
19. The Purpose and Pursuit of Focus: The Book of Nehemiah (Chapters 1-4)

Acknowledgements

There are so many people that I wish to acknowledge and I really don't know where to start. I need to save God for last because I must give him the proper honor due to him. I would like to thank every reader that has chosen to pick up this book, buy it, believe in the words that are written, decide to make a decision and trust in their own process to Start Over, and Love It.

I give great honor to the many friends that have helped me completely hold it together over the last 5 years: Gina Dacus, Verilyn Radford Bellamy, Stephanie Ross, Kelsi Arceaneaux, Tamara Steele, Tiffany James, and Angela Hall. I so appreciate all of you for your tireless efforts in ensuring that I was well mentally, spiritually and many times financially. I promise it will not be in vain.

To my new found friends and sisters who I have met in the recent years, but it seems like an eternity, I applaud you and thank you for speaking into my life and allowing the divine connection of God to ensure success in our friendship: Lisa Smith, Sukari Beshears, Chaunna Layton, Nicole Caldwell, Justina Okoh, Lenesha Toney, Leticia Evans and Inga Mork. Our times together have been the best and forever cherished moments in my life, giving breathe of life to what at times felt like death of living.

I would like to thank Dr. Carrie Frazier, who served as my Clinical Supervisor, mentor, and advisor during some difficult times and while collecting my counseling hours. You are truly a breathe of fresh air. To Ms. Gloria Hartsough, Founder of Parents, Partners and Providers for Educating Young Children. You really believed in my come back by allowing me to do my clinical work and other classes at your facility, and for that I will FOREVER be indebted.

There are two more women that I would like to acknowledge is Mary K. Thomas, for keeping me focused on who I am, and where God has brought me from, and where he is going to take me too. Thank you so much Mrs. Thomas for believing in me since the 1st grade as a 5 year old talkative little girl at Stevenson Elementary School. You said that one day, my mouth would lead me to do great things, and I think you are right.

Lastly, but not least, Pastor Christine Liddell, who was my Pastor for 8 years at Power For Living Ministries. Truly you have been consistent throughout these 12 years of knowing me, and I am honored to have been able to learn from you, grow, and able to see the reflection of God's light in your life.

You helped to make my "Starting Over", true, purposeful, God sent, and confirming and for that I am so grateful and forever indebted. Thank you so much as you were a serious piece to me making some very real steps to my now place.

There are so many other woman that I could thank God for, but I love you all, even if I didn't name you, please know that I love you.

I am totally not obligated to only thanking the women in my life, but there are some great brothers and men who have made sure that they were available, and up for the challenge (whatever I had going on), to be present in my Starting Over process and so I would like to acknowledge Elder Ron Rosson who provided a platform for me to do what I love to do: Worship The King through Song and Speech, Minister Duwaun King, for always being a real brother at all times, so I thank you both.

To Reverand Terrell Turner, for allowing the gift of God, and inspired messages to impart hope, spiritual help and healing to seek for God beyond the norm, and stretch beyond my natural capacity, thank you.

Lastly, I would like to thank is Mr. Roman Curtis, who as my landlord during the time of this book being printed and published, sincerely believed in the promise that God had over my life, and trusted that it would all eventually come together.

Lastly but not least, to God, my father and savior. I cry even at the writing of this, because I know had you not been true to your word, in keeping me, guiding me and protecting me, I just don't think this might have happened. You allowed things to happen and then block other things from happening, and for that I am so very grateful.

Truly God your word is my rock and your spirit is my guide, and your frequent check-ins with me allowed me to believe in me again. I thank you SIR for being the almighty King, one that is tangible, yet relatable, flexible, yet firm, and absolutely lovable. I pray that I make you proud, for you are the reason, why I breathe!

Lakita D. Long
Antioch, CA

Preface

This book came about as a result of a decision that I made 13 years ago, and the delay in my responding and acting upon what I knew was true at that time.

This starting over process was and has not been easy, and truly I did not love it, thus it has taken me actually 3 years to finish this book, because it was important that I got to a real place of "loving it" so that I can be true and authentic in the delivery of this process.

While this book has been in the making for several years, it has truly been a central theme in my life period. The ability to start over, and love it! Whether it was a job, a failed business, relationship, or project, starting over is just something I have had to do. But I found out that you can have so many of these "starting over" moments that stifles who you are, and tries to delay your process of finishing what you started.

As I finally got to the place where I can face myself, my situation, and make it known that I have to make some radical changes in my life, the vision for the work "Starting Over and Loving It", became much more clearer.

I hope that as you read through the pages, should you find yourself in the same situation that you would take hold to God's grace for your life, and decide that you will be begin to embrace these transitions and love the process, least you stay stuck and stagnate, and angry for far too long, producing lack of fruit and the inability to move forward.

Therefore, I have included a *Change Your Life Reflection Moment*, that gives you time to review what the chapter was about and make it more personal to your own situation.

Even if you are divorce, financially broke, broken hearted, or very successful people can and do get an opportunity to start over, and I pray that this book is used as a tool of encouragement, empowerment and a gentle reminder to you that you can still make the choice to Start Over and Love It!

Introduction

Ecclesiastes 3:3:1
"To every thing there is a season, and a time to every purpose under the heaven"

Starting Over, for me began more than 3 years ago, but it was long and difficult and felt like a lifetime, until I started to love the process. There were so many factors involved, and yet I had to believe from the outset that I would indeed come through this.

Most of people's ability to start over means they need to just keep going. Robert Frost an American Literary figure highly regarded for his realistic depictions of rural life and his command of American colloquial speech says this about life, "It can be summed up in three words, It Goes On".

If we do not resolve to keep moving forward even when we are hurting, we may lose the complete drive to even stay in this life. I have only known a few people to personally take their life, but that image leaves a gaping hole in my soul and heart about the human will and how it bends to life's issues. We are all susceptible to it.

While trying to keep myself afloat, I walked through a lot of crap and stuff that just sucked. But if I am truthful I also had the wonderful privilege of experiencing a lot of great things, meeting a lot of wonderful people, and for that alone I am grateful.

I am sure that my good things outweighed the bad, but in the moment it was not detected. What did come up was various scriptures from the bible, which gave comfort in knowing that I would come out of this.

One particular verse in ***Jeremiah 29: 11***, which says, *"For I know the thoughts that I think toward you, saith the Lord, thoughts of peace, and not of evil, to give you an expected end."* I needed to know that God's thoughts truly surpassed what I was walking through, because my situation looked very bleak, even when I changed perspectives.

As I continue to find refugee in God's word, I held on to ***Psalm 138:8***, which says, *"The Lord will perfect that which concerneth me: thy mercy, O Lord, endureth for ever; forsake not the works of thine own hands."* God will not forsake the works that is in me, but I needed to really believe this, and something deep down inside suggested that I did not.

Throughout the book I am hoping that while I share my story you will find the peace, comfort and spiritual uplifting that is found in God's word. I believe that all things indeed work together for your good, and even while the tears stream down your face, or the frustration mounts against your efforts, I have prayed for each reader, and believe that God's healing is totally available for you.

I pray that each chapter leaves you not so much focusing on my story, but more on the power of God to deliver you out of your story. This book is for divorcees, singles, married, man, woman, black, white, rich or poor. It doesn't matter where you find yourself on the spectrum, Starting Over can be an essential part of your life, and increase the longevity of your life and renew purpose, vigor and your life's assignment.

As I have pulled the information from the depths of my core, and put it in a format that would be inspiring, I hope you are as encouraged as I was by writing it to know that your best life has yet to be lived. You are at your finest moments, and as soon as you get what it is you are suppose to be doing, and you stick to that one thing, then you will be satisfied, fulfilled, and completely content.

To **Start Over,** is to have a new mindset about the way that you are going to live out your life. **Starting Over** holds nothing back, but exposes all of your flaws, insecurities assets and liabilities to your creator, so that healing and wholeness takes place, and the fruit and joy of living comes back into your soul.

While we can not hit the physical reset button on our life, we can be reborn in the spirit. Such is the conversation between the religious leader Nicodemus and Jesus, when he asked, *"how can a man be born again when he is old? Can he enter the second time into his mother's womb, and be born?"* Jesus said, *"verily, verily, I say unto thee, except a man be born of water and of the Spirit, he cannot enter into the Kingdom of God"* John 3:4-5

Our *Starting Over* is not a mere physical one with tangible needs outwardly, but it is a spiritual one, that constitutes the inner workings of our hearts, minds, soul and spirit. We need an inner change that would allow us to see everything in our lives appropriately.

I urge you to enjoy the ride, open up your heart to the many experiences, quotes, scriptures, moments in time that will at least encourage you to know that you can indeed Start Over and Love it!

Remember you were made for this time, and now is the season to **Relaunch** your hopes, dreams, and life's purpose, and do what it is that you were called to do. Never doubt the need to put one foot in front of the other.

As a favorite quote of mines that I say to myself, "change only happens when what you no is no longer good enough". Perfect where you are, and trust the process. You aren't the first person to go through what you went through and you will unfortunately not be the last.

Smile and *Start Over and Love it!*

SECTION ONE: The Backdrop

Chapter One

THE BACKDROP:
A Brief Look at the Beginning

"What the hell is going on, how could this be happening, how did I get here, and why am I here this long?" These were the internal thoughts I had almost everyday for more than 3 years, while trying to rediscover who I was and getting back to where I thought that I needed to be.

So here I am sharing about a story that was only real because I lived it and have too many reminders that let me know that I indeed was there.

To give you a better sense of the full story, I wanted to give you the backdrop and look at the beginning, and then bring you current. This will hopefully allow you to trace your own steps of how you started, and where and when you went astray from the purposed plan that you intended.

I am an advocate that "change only happens when what you know is no longer good enough", therefore I believe that all beginnings can have a great ending. So let's take a look at the beginning of how this all got started.

The time is February 2000, and I am in the prime of everything I know, and in a very good space in my life. I finished graduate school with a Masters degree in Counseling, was being used as an Evangelist to minister in many different places way outside the borders of the traditional church, worked full time, had a successful consulting practice, bought a new car and was really enjoying my life.

Then there was a call from someone that wanted to utilize my Professional Services of providing organizational development to their newly formed expansion of their business. Till this day, I don't know how they even got my information as I hadn't met them before.

The company that called me was a local record label with major named artist and they were embarking upon many different projects and wanted to see if I could come to one of their meetings, and see if I could help steer them organizational, as there were so many new partners involved, and they wanted to keep everything straight. I arrived at the meeting sat down in this semi-circle, everyone introduced themselves, and the guy that called me verbally highlighted my work again after I said who I was, and we moved forward.

The guy who called me, I will call his name Matthew, toward the end of the meeting, said that he thought that I really needed to work with this one group and their label as they could really use my services of getting organized, and to be able to do it quickly because that group was the one that had the "hot new artist" coming in.

Well at the time, I was about doing business, and getting my money, so I wasn't going to turn down any money, but when the person step back into the room that he wanted me to work with, there was a CAUTION in my spirit. Something immediately vexed me. But I shook hands, and the guy who I will call Bobby, gave me his card, and asked for mine. Said the nice things and then talked for a few minutes, and left.

In hindsight, I realized that while I was called to the main group to do work, I sensed early on that they wanted me to really help this Bobby, but maybe even "watch" him. The events were strange to me, but I then said it is just business and moved on.

Later on that night Bobby called me, but I didn't answer, as I felt that CAUTION thing again, and just went on with my night. Well he continued to call and page me, and I would send back information via page, or email, but he was very eager to want to TALK to me. But I was busy.

Now we are in April of 2000, and still he is calling much more, almost in this needy way, and I did not understand because I had did all the work that he needed done via email and faxing, because he kept having a different motive, when he would talk with me, first about business, and staying on track...which I was glad about but then at the end trying to talk personal stuff, which I would say I have to go, I have another client waiting.

But over a period of time about a month, everything we talked about was business, and I was like yes, finally he gets it, so when he asked if we could do a business lunch, I didn't think anything of it. We met at Everett and Jones in Oakland, CA and had the meeting.

During this meeting I felt that he was trying to get something else done, but it wasn't what was on our agenda. Then he asked, "would you be interested in being a partner in my label"? This is what the uneasiness was about. I declined, and said that I was just too busy, because it really just felt not right, rushed but pre-planned on his part.

I suspected that he gathered in our conversation that I love to speak, and teach, and had a real love for peoples personal and profession development, so he thought he would ask. I felt that this was a good time to get up and leave the lunch, and let him know that I had to go. So he stated okay, I am walking this way (to the car garage), and said I can walk you to your car. I said you don't have to, he said no that is fine, it would be my honor.

As we are walking he tells me right off the bat, "I have 3 girls" and I was like so taken aback, because I was like "where did that come from"? I said you definitely have your hands full, and he said yes I do, but they are living with their mom. Another "uh oh" in my spirit—baggage is what I thought. This was just too much already. So I jumped in my car and sped off.

Several months later, still getting the calls but too busy to respond to them because I started to feel "stalked", and I just didn't want to even do business anymore. The last time I spoke with him, it was a conversation that went something like, "hey let's just be about the business, and move forward".

Then in August 2000, I kept getting these pages from a number I did not recognize, but I have seen before because some of my clients that I worked with in the City of Oakland had the same prefix and it looked like their number.

On my break from teaching Introduction to Sociology class, I called it back and it was this Bobby guy again, and I immediately told him that I thought that it was a client of mine, and he quickly said that the work that I did with and for him paid off, as he now had an office in Eastmont Mall, and things were moving forward.

Great, I thought, what a wonderful thing to add to my testimonials. He then said, "can you stop by here so you can see it, and while still feeling the CAUTION, pride and ego was like "yeah" go and see it.

I looked down at my hand, and was glad that I wore my "stay away I'm involved with someone diamond ring" so I was good to go. After work, I left Santa Clara, and headed to Oakland but something wasn't right. Although I had not heard from him on my business number (because he lost it I later found out), there was a check in my spirit.

So I arrived there and the place was somewhat in a disarray, but not like someone just moved into the place, kinda like someone was in the position of moving out. So I said, "great move, still looks like you have some more things to put together". He quickly starting talking about this and that, and then I reached out to shake his hand, and he says, "oh I see someone beat me to it (notices the diamond ring on my ring finger), and I said, yeah something like that.

Well, I would love to celebrate with you and take you out to eat, can I call you? In my mind, I said, oh he is asking now, thinking this is why he hasn't called. I said sure, but my best friend is going to be out here visiting so she will have to come with us.

He asked if he could call me, and I said sure let me know when. But he says, I don't have your number, and I said, "I'm so sorry I am not going to give it to you again". He starts rattling off a partial of the number, all but the last two, so I help him out and left.

While everything in me screamed wrong, no, I felt that I had let him in my space, and my pride made me believe that I had enough wherewithal to do things the way that I wanted, but I had no idea that I would be like a prey of what felt like an "emotional predator".

The moment that contact came, and the constant talking on the phone, I just starting losing stuff. My car, which was not even a month behind 22 days late payment, money gone, tired, conflicted, extremely overwhelmed, and this is happening and there is no sexual contact going on. It was merely conversation, talking, which is a form of deep connecting, and intimacy.

But I knew what it was and felt trapped! I was getting deeper and deeper and after a few months, I had enough, and I broke it off, but not before a very ugly public not so good argument, where I felt threatened, and had made up my mind enough.

So after walking away from the argument, I walked away from the relationship and did not talk with him for almost 10 months, nor thought about him, and just as fast as I lost everything, that is how fast I got it back. Visited other countries first class, ministering, and the excitement and Joy of the Lord had returned. I had a new lease on life.

But then the call came in the Summer of 2001. Bobby called me asking if I had plans for Fourth of July, and I did, and he said well I wanted to say hello, and to see if you wanted to come by. I said thank you but no thanks, I am not available. But he called 3 more times I was like irritated, because I didn't even like being around his family. Nothing personal, it just didn't work.

In hindsight, I ended up going, because I think I wanted to see if maybe he was different, even though my gut told me he was still the same person, and keep my distance.

At the very least, I had to reckon with myself that he was not even my type, and I did not want a guy with kids, and there was too much unknown stuff, and I always felt wildly overwhelmed by his life. Even though I was not lonely, desperate, I went, and it was horrible. I realized that his constant "wearing me down", excessively calling, buttering up etc. was meant to look like "I really want you there", but it had the signs of an "emotional stalker".

An "emotional stalker" is where a person will go through great lengths to stalk someone they want. That person becomes the object of their affection but they don't necessarily really want them, but it is the chase, the thrill and the other hidden motives.

An *emotional stalker*, has stalked someone for at least 3 times before, and although they go hard for the relationships, once the person realizes what they have the end the relationship and they guy/girl ends the relationship and becomes fearful of losing their identity and self-worth and desperately wants to re-establish the dominance and control that they formed in the relationship.

But this time, I think he is different because his interaction is different, and I think, "oh he has learned", but in the back of my mind, I am still irritated that he kept calling, and the thought that he has 3 kids with two different ladies was just too much. I did not know that this was all apart of the game. Whether he consciously played it or not, I went along with something that was not me and it lessened my internal alarms for danger and eventually would lessen the value for myself.

It seemed like years of "good times" passed but in fact it was just months and he then proposed, told me to think about it and that he was paying on a ring. I told him I can not marry you, I have too many doubts, and so many things are just not right.

Some additional months passed by and now we have been dating on and off in my heart, but to him consistently. We had visited this ring store, while window shopping and he asked me "if you could have a ring, what would you want?". Because I was not "there" in mind about marriage, I pointed to a very beautiful 1 Carat Diamond ring. Then we left and came back to the Bay.

Some months went by, he asked me, "have you thought about being my fiancée?" I said, "thinking but not ready to do anything." In more conversations he starts to ask a lot of "what if" questions". What if I was everything you wanted me to be, we were compatible, I am spiritual, and could fully provide for you, would you be my fiancée with the goal of being my wife? Well all these questions, and long conversations, started to feel like something else, and when I saw it, I felt trapped.

One day he calls and says I want to take you to dinner, and take a ride out to Burlingame with me, which is where the restaurant is. I said okay, and I wait for him to come.

We go out to eat, and then we leave the restaurant and he arranges for me to go and get my nails done at this shop. I do thinking that was nice of him. Then he comes back and picks me up and we go get in the car.

While sitting in the car, he pulls out this small black box, and he is acting kinda nervous when he is talking, and then he looks and opens the box, and says, "Lakita will you marry me". It was unreal, somewhat exciting but I felt like I couldn't said no, so I overrode the fact that I was just not there, and said YES. I then stated to him but I can't do it anytime soon. So much excitement, but so many other feelings too, but I the bottom line was I still said yes.

I later learned that my saying yes, when I really didn't want to would be tied to my long standing inability to have clear boundaries with people that seemed okay but I knew was not good and true for my life. For some reason I felt like I "owed" him a yes because I kept him waiting. Or was it because throughout our "long talks" on the phone, he was sublimely planting this in my head, "that I owed him something". This would be a big truth, and a constant thing throughout the relationship, and a form of control that would be hard to break.

Change Your Life Reflection Moment

Now you have read my *Backdrop, A Brief Look At The Beginning*, and seen at a very brief but real level some of the initial things that went very wrong:

1. Going against warning in my spirit
2. The fact that I felt stalked (has meaning)
3. There was no real reason or starting point to how I even got connected to him
4. Felt threatened and out of sorts, and publicly humiliated
5. Choosing someone who was totally not my type at all. Everything was wrong about him.
6. Know God, but never went to God for the full answers. When I did, it would prove to be what I thought was too late.
7. I said yes, and everything in me said NO

When you open up your soul and spirit illegally, it creates so many strongholds, not to mention any of the things that you might have brought in yourself. Sometimes you don't feel strong enough to just walk away, because it seems to attach itself and never let go. But there is liberty in God, and when you call upon him in your distress.

Here are a few questions to ask yourself:

1. So what's your **BACKDROP**, and how are you ensuring that you aren't going through that cycle again?

It is within your power to rewrite your life's story by the power of the Holy Spirit. Don't let your beginning be your end. Think about the things that you said yes to, that clearly the Holy Spirit was saying no to. Make a decision to review your story and choose the next chapter.

Chapter Two

Growing Wearing, Staying In Place

So throughout my engagement process I am going through the motions, and a lot is going on in my head. At times, I am feeling okay with it, and other times I am not doing so well. But now I felt like I have something to prove until another opportunity presents itself, and I can "legitimately" get away.

Even though I could have just walked away I was going back to that old (childhood) self pattern of sabotaging things, where, I punished myself, because I felt like, "I should have known better". And even though that opportunity would present itself several times over a period of time, I still stayed in place.

So what does it mean to grow weary? And why stay in place where things are not good? *Weary* means to be physically or mentally exhausted by hard work, exertion, strain, fatigue or tired. When you are weary you are impatient or dissatisfied easily and because it comes out in the same setting in which it was produced you don't know what to do with it.

Here I was still struggling, losing stuff, time and feeling anxious, because this engagement was too far in, and just not right even when things were right. Kept wearing the ring for almost a year in a half and then something happens……

One Saturday while working at the Clinic in San Leandro, California, the person who answers the front desk says, Lakita the call is for you. I was thinking, "I have a cell phone, so who could this be, to not know to call me from there. I looked on my phone and realized that I ignored a call from someone with an area code of 530.

I answered and said this is Lakita, how can I help you? The voice on the other end of the phone said, "hi, I am Officer Stanton* and your "husband" was speeding and was pulled over and he was not able to get a hold of you, so we let him use the phone to call you, so you would know what is going on. I was like, "what, husband".

He proceeded to tell me that his brother who was also with him will be driving the rest of the way, and that while he was pulled over for a traffic situation, he actually had several warrants out for his arrest. Oh Lord, what is going on? What are the warrants for?

A thump in my throat, chest, mind, head had happened all at once; then Bobby my fiancée got on the phone and started saying thank you for taking my call and proceeded to tell me all that was going on in a matter of face way, or rather that it will be "all cleared up" really soon.

At this time I am sick, because I don't have this type of stuff in my life, and he lied. The first thing I asked him was, "why did you tell him I was your wife? Why didn't you just tell him the truth?" He said, "because they would not have given me the call".

Whether or not that was true I did not care, and asked, "why didn't you call your mom?". He said that his brother would tell her. In fact I found out that he indeed did call her too. Then he says, "I should be out of here soon, but if you don't want to continue on in this relationship I would understand".

Okay, world wind just happened and was all too much, too soon, which increased my weariness. So I went silent on the phone. Had I been a different color, people would have seen me change colors probably 5 times. I didn't know what was going on, but it didn't feel right, but I stayed.

Got off the phone and although I felt one way about the situation, I told my boss who was also a friend, something slightly different *(the bold me talking, stating that I was done and thought that I should probably get out of this relationship)*. I didn't lie, I just had a little more optimism and made the big things seem very small, but she reminded me that I have been kinda wanting to get out and here was my chance.

So I sat there, at her desk and listened to her say, "maybe this is it. You will be free and able to go on with your life. Really who speeds, gets pulled over and taken to jail on old warrants, someone who evaded the law". I sat and listened, but my pride was injured, ego distorted, and shame of even getting involved was taking over my rational and the CAUTION that the Lord kept pressing upon me.

Immediately I thought what will I tell the PEOPLE. Oh that was just too much to bare. At this point, my mind had gotten into the "what would be" point if everything worked out, and so now, much was invested but at the end of the day it was still PRIDE.

So I left my office, exhausted, because now I am working overtime in my head, trying to figure out how I was going to tell the story when people asked where was my fiancée? I thought to myself, well it is innocent enough, to get pulled over for speeding, have some warrants, and do a couple of days in jail. I will just tell them a truthful, yet not full story of this version. But something was troubling me.

The conversation and the tone of the Officer gave me reason to believe otherwise. My weariness was now starting to cause my decisions to be not clear, and yet I stayed in place. But there was more....

Bobby calls me and I was nervous because I didn't know what the information was going to be. I was hoping he was going to tell me that it was nothing, but that was not the case.

He ended up telling me that the warrants were related to some old cases of his "old cases" what, and that while he was on probation during that time, he was told as apart of his original sentencing that he could not go out of the area without permission even to live, but he did not, so they put warrants out for him. He kept saying he was going to get out in one week, but weeks went by and turned into a year and 2 months.

I begin to shrink, and he was writing me letters, just all too much. While he stated that he understood if I moved on, I never believed it, and because of my need to "fix things, and the project that I started", I stayed, weary and all.

Really in light of it all, he wanted access to my emotions and to see how "far away I was getting" from him. This is what "*emotional predators*" do. While he was giving me the option "to leave" the relationship it was not really an option, because he had already worked on my mind through conversation and now in the letters that would suggest other things. This is true for him and usually true for emotional predators.

Emotional predators are characterized by preying on the emotions of people who they feel has already shown them vulnerability. They use compulsive lying, have multiple sexual partners, lead secret double lives, control by any means even in nice ways, threats that come off as jokes, stalking, violence (verbal or physical), emotional abuse and play mind games. They constantly convince people around them that they are okay only to gain access to their space and life.

Do you know some emotional predators? Please rest assure that this process that I am talking about is less about the people and more about our process of why we even let them in our space in the first place.

Emotional predators will stop at nothing, have the traits and characteristics of a narcissistic person. They are neither gender specific, nor is it based on ethnic origin. These traits have been evident in the persons life for a long time, but family members have made their "bad behaviors" be just who they are.

So now, I am totally feeling an unwarranted pressure to stay in something that is not what I want and I am growing more weary, fatigued of getting out of this. Everything crazy, feeling free, but hindered, and not really free because as he was due to come out, another charge was found in another County and he begged me to help his defense attorney get the information or else he was going to have to do a lot of real time 5 to 7 years.

So I moved into action, because I didn't want to see him do that, nor did I want to have to further explain more jail time; pride was fully in effect, it was not about him at all, but about me.

I found the information that could possibly clear his name and gave it to the defense attorney, and it proved to be true, so then I felt entrapped by "the good parts" that I saw, and the glimmer of truth that I felt, moved me forward.

Change Your Life Reflection Moment

Now that you have read about *Growing Weary, Staying In Place*, have you done this too? Have you been exhausted, fatigued, overwhelmed but stayed in the same place?

Weary implies being weary? Being physically or mentally exhausted by hard work, exertion, strain, etc.; fatigued; tired. Weary is characterized by or causes fatigue as in a journey. Weariness means that you are impatient or dissatisfied with something and easily irked by things.

1. What are you weary (physically or mentally exhausted) by?
2. Are you working on things, or in relationships with people that fatigues you, and you become easily impatient?
3. Are you staying in place, because you don't know where to go?
4. Is the thing that is not normal, becoming your norm?
5. Do you have emotional predators in your life? If so who are they? Are you one?

Chapter Three

The Argument and the Accident Before the Wedding

Everything that could go wrong did go wrong. We were still feuding about a lot of things, and mainly things that I wanted to see him do before I said I do. He felt that I was holding his past too much in the present, and I reminded him that it wasn't too long ago that he got out of jail and that I had every right to be wanting to make sure that he is right, and straight.

This continued on and off for months, and we went to pre-martial counseling, broke off the wedding 3 months before it was scheduled, and walked out of pre-martial counseling. Just too much, and that is not the testimony that I wanted, nor did I plan for my life, but I was invested already 4 years, and I think I felt like something good needed to come out of this.

The arguments continued into the month of April 2004, which was about the fact that I wanted to push the wedding back another year, or at least until December of 2004. He didn't want to do that since he felt that a 3 year engagement was long enough. I brought up all these other issues, work, money, his kids everything. So things got more heated, because I just did not want to move forward.

Besides the fact that we had these similar yet smaller arguments before, we were now into a serious disagreement in late April just 2 months before the wedding, in which I would find myself so stressed that I got into my brand new car, and headed towards Riverside only to get into a serious car accident on Highway 5.

All I remembered prior to the accident was that he said one thing, I said another and I was angry, because I hadn't figured out how to tell him no I don't want to marry you, and was not sure why, but I stormed out of my house, told him to lock my door when he left, and jumped on the freeway. Then I started shaking, did I cause this accident?

But as it would be, as I was driving, a small mini van in front of me slowed up for no reason then stopped, hit its brakes, hit the car in front of it I slammed into the back of it after it flipped over. Just a mess, and I was scared, and I realized that I was a complete nervous wreck.

So the CHP came, and another driver stopped, because they saw everything, and we saw the latino guy banged up, in the car but when it was time to check on the person in the minivan, the man was gone. He just disappeared. I think he went into the vineyards that were on the right, possibly because he was undocumented. I don't know why he was gone, but he was gone. Did you hear me just vanished in the night.

So now I am really freaking out. My car was a mess, and I was on my way to my mom's as we were giving her a party and so I called my brother Ivan to see what I should do. He said call the insurance, and then if you can make it down here do so.

I don't know how I made it down there, but I did, and I still had over 200 miles to drive from where the accident originally happened. My insurance company told me where I could go in the area where I was, and that I could leave my car, and get a rental car to drive. Was this a warning from God? I didn't know, but it sure felt not right.

Bobby called me to see if I made it to Riverside okay, and I said yes, but I got into a car accident on the way, and it was pretty bad. He was like what happened, trying to be concerned, but I was angry; at myself. Not at him, at myself. He kept trying to console me, and I thanked him and told him I would call him later.

The argument would prove to be a serious sign of things to come, and a precursor of many of the events that would take place over the course of 10 years. I would survive it, but I would be scarred emotionally and on edge, not making things better for a smooth transition into the wedding or marriage.

Boy where was all of this going?

Change Your Life Reflection Moment

Now that you have read about *The Argument and the Accident Before The Wedding?* Maybe it is not a wedding for you, but I am sure that you have found yourself in a heated discussion with someone that you care about, and it distorted your thinking momentarily possibly causing you to do something you had no business doing.? Well in order to Start Over and Love It you must open up to the mishaps that take place, because of misplaced anger.

Such was the case for me. An argument is an oral disagreement; verbal opposition; contention; altercation: which is a violent argument. It is also a discussion involving differing points of view; debate and is noted as a process of reasoning; series of reasons. So what is going on in you that feels like an ongoing argument

1. What are you weary (physically or mentally exhausted) by?
2. Are you working on things, or in relationships with people that fatigues you, and you become easily impatient?
3. Are you staying in place, because you don't know where to go?
4. Is the thing that is not normal, becoming your norm?
5. Do you have emotional predators in your life? If so who are they? Are you one?

Chapter Four

The Wedding and Being At Home

So now it is the time for the wedding, the event of the year, but everything kept happening, up until the day. I had my wedding in a church that seated 700 people, sent out 450 invitations 250 came, so the place looked rather emptied and I was somewhat sad and perplexed.

I wrote a song that ended up being literally made on the spot, but it flowed, and fit, and was so nice, so I felt like "wow" this is good. The music to the song I had, but the words literally felt right and good as it reflected a story of the funny parts of the courting and dating, and it had some symbolic thought of love. Because in spite of it all, I believed that I loved him, or maybe I was in love with the idea of being loved?

During the reception there was irritation in the atmosphere from my family side, as they were not still convinced that this was truly something that I should have moved forward with but it was too late now, we were soon going to be walking in what is called "oneness".

In hindsight, I had some of my friends in my wedding but really none was in complete agreement about it, so the process didn't have the "real" feeling of getting married. Like it didn't exist.

The wedding was over as fast as it started and I realized in the end that, we didn't have a videographer, the photographer we had was someone he know, and albeit he was a photographer, but I think he left professionalism at home, and did not take enough photos at all.

It was almost like the wedding never happened. Bobby and I had no photos together, just wrong and while some things "kinda" came to together, the mood was not festive enough to me.

One of my friends who I asked to be in my wedding said that she could not be in it and stated that, while she loved me, she did not support the union, and I respected her for that, but it made me think about the isolation that I was possibly setting myself up for, and while she came, everything still seemed off.

Got into the hotel in Lafayette, California and Bobby got in the shower, excited about having sex and spending time with me and I was sitting on the bed in my wedding gown balling, because I felt like I made the worst mistake in my life, and said outloud, "what have I done?" I know I cared for him, and probably even loved him, but my mind and heart was still double minded in this because everything that I didn't want is what he was and I was not truthful with him about this.

While being with someone creates a comfort level, my spirit could not get settled, but I started to tell my mind and heart that I needed to move on with life, and go for it, things would get better.

39

But now it was my hope and desire that he would actually do what he said he would do, so that I would not have to face the inevitable truth, that I allowed my pride and fear of what the people would think override the truth of what I knew, I have disobeyed the prompting of the Holy Spirit, and what I really wanted.

Now he was my husband, and I think I convinced myself that I could actually change him even though I never said it, and although I masked it as God will do it, I was sure hoping that I could "help" in some way, like I did in so many other things.

The next day we left for Hawaii for the honeymoon for 7 days, and argued a lot and while on the trip he was still receiving business calls (real estate, closing deals), I tried to be more and more supportive but the calls increased more and more and we had a talk about how I felt. The truth of the matter was that I did not want to be married, and could have probably argued about anything. He was sympathetic, listened we made up and I moved on.

After the trip, his life is in full gear, and so is mine. We came back home, and he said that we needed to start looking for us a house to buy. So we started looking and six months after we got married we bought our first house and it was done in a traditional way. We borrowed $10,000 from his mom, and then put money down on the house, paid her back, and moved into our first house. This begin some of the great times the many great times together.

With the wedding over, now comes the time to being at home, and dealing with each other on a daily basis. Something I really hadn't anticipated. What, your married girl, get a clue? This was something that I felt was going to take some time getting use to and I needed to try my best, but I had no models.

At Home

Now I am married, I am here, and I needed to try and put my best foot forward, and go for it. Time to be at home and live this married life which I came to find out quick fast and in a hurry that it was not easy at all, but I was going to have to get it together.

The really coming together was not happening fast enough, and in November of that first year of marriage (2004) just a few months of being married, I typed a 10 page email letter, stating that I have talked with an attorney and think that we need to annul this marriage. He went off on me, and it did more than frighten me, it warned me and reminded me of the CAUTION that I felt when he was first pursuing me.

Needless to say, I started to intentionally fall asleep downstairs, and it got so bad that it was just unbearable to be there. So after one of our heated discussions, I stormed out of the house, needing to get to work in Oakland, and on November 19, 2004, I would get into yet another terrifying car accident in the same car, I had an accident in earlier. This time my car almost went over the embankment on Highway 4. If the impact was a little bit more and different type car, I might not be writing this book.

I immediately called him, was shaking because now this is the second time that I am in an accident after an argument with him, how I left and where I was emotionally. So now I don't know what to think. To make matters worst was the major contract that I had been working for two years, was suddenly at least to me, was drying up, but it I thought that it could have lasted for 3 years. Now I felt like I was losing myself. And all his stuff was starting to come together.

Despite many emotionally painful nights, there were many, many good times. Times where I was able to breathe, and then I wondered if any of what I thought was true or right. We repented to each other, and for a time and a season it was working, but if you keep taking back your repented heart, then you become divided within.

Working Together

Then he asked if I would help him doing some of the trainings, and some of the marketing stuff for his company which was starting to gain traction. So after getting over all that I felt, I said yes. Gave some suggestions to him, he liked it, put it into action and trainings that originally brought in 25 people, starting bringing in 200, then within 1 year in a half jumped from $0 net worth, to $15 million dollars, but as you know many things happen when money is involved, especially lots of it.

Things started being super fast paced, and time together started to feel more like a partnership in a company rather than husband and wife. I also sensed that one of the young ladies working my husband liked him, but he shrugged it off, saying "no she doesn't like me."

But then one time he was having a meeting with some of his staff at our house and I decided to come back early just to see everyone, and I parked on the street, so the garage would not open and she was there. I expected other team members, but there was no one but him and her there. When I walked in the look on his face was like this is awkward and she was way too friendly. Totally uncomfortable at this point for him and me, but that night my husband said you know maybe you are right, she might have liked me but I didn't see her that way.

We are at home gaining momentum in our relationship, being known as a power couple, doing stuff in the church, building the businesses that we had, purchased a fitness gym franchise, and a host of other businesses, things were looking great.

Then in the summer of 2005 I had to go on a ministry trip to Chicago, and scheduled to have my family reunion at my house with all of my family staying at my house, and when I came back, I noticed that my size 10 skirt was tight, and I hadn't had my monthly yet. Nervous and annoyed, I did not want to be pregnant, because we had just celebrated our first anniversary, and was finally getting a little bit of a groove.

Pregnancy

I took one pregnancy test, and sure enough it said positive. The next day, my family was coming so I told my husband, hey I have something to tell you, and he said what is it, and I said, I think that I am pregnant. There was a pause, not really excited, and I felt rejected, because his face said it all, "I don't want another kid".

I then tried to hide the hurt I felt and said, it probably was not accurate, so it is nothing, and I walked away. I thought how insensitive. Like I wanted to have a baby, and I was on the pill. I went and cried, and he found me, and said, "hey I wasn't trying to hurt your feelings but I just wasn't expecting that, and was really excited, but was kinda like not right now". I heard him but it didn't make me feel better, so I got up to do the last little bit of stuff for my family arrival 20 deep in my house.

While we had made it, house, cars, influence, money, and everything else we were still not emotionally synchronized as one, or spiritually for that matter but I did not have time to be thinking about that as my family would be flying in from everywhere, and there was much to do.

When they arrived I was a little down, because I had just planned to get a Harley Davidson Bike, and now I am pregnant. So when my niece arrives, I asked her if she would go to the store with me, and I got two more pregnancy tests, and took them back to back, and yes, I was indeed pregnant.

I didn't understand it, but there was tension in the air, because my husband did not want anymore children right away, remember he had three, and we had just gotten married, it was all too much.

But then out of the blue while everyone is in the living my husband says, hey family Lakita has something to say. What? I don't have anything to say, so I quickly said, "hey everybody, I want you to enjoy yourself, this home is your home for the week. If there is anything that I can do to make your stay better let me know". But he looked at me, and said, "tell them". I just couldn't believe it. It was so non-emotional, insensitive and I hadn't even processed it. I told him that I wanted to wait a while before sharing, as it had only been 48 hours since I found out.

I was so angry, and this would be the beginning of him not adhering to my wishes. So I tell them, and my mother quickly discerns that something is not right. Rather than my family be excited for me, they just had blank stares.

This was probably due to the timing, and the fact that all of my life, I did not want to have children, although I was great with them. I never talked about them, and yet again another unplanned thing, yet in God's eyes, it was planned.

At this point I am feeling dismissed and disregarded. Both are words that have serious meanings to me, and maybe like some of you that have words that trigger certain reactions these definitely did at the time.

To be *dismiss* is to direct or tell someone to go. It is to allow or give permission or a request to depart. It also means to discharge or remove from an office or service. It gives way to the feeling of discard or reject and that is exactly how I felt.

The situation and the way he responded made me feel disregarded (probably because it was not the first time he had done this). To be *disregarded* means to pay no attention to; leave out of consideration; ignore and to treat without due regard, respect, or attentiveness.

At times and too often in relationships we ignore real issues and it creates great dissonance within us and we disconnect, feeling fragmented trying to figure out where you are with people, but if you listen closely you will find out where you are with people.

So my first baby girl was here, and I had the most uncomfortable, stressful pregnancy. As the income increases, the responsibility does, and so does the stress, and ironically the uncertainty of the future as a couple because something was stained in my heart and soul from past verbal attacks and abuse that up until this point I didn't even acknowledge. I had severe lows during pregnancy, various forms of depression, and just craziness.

The arguments escalated, and the disagreements harbored a feeling of resentment within me. I felt ravished emotionally and was being fought on every end for him to have his two older children come and live with us.

We discussed this once before, and I asked if he could give me at least 6 months to have the baby and then get acquainted with her, and we could have them to live with us. But no, he ended up picking them up from Reno, even though he said he was just going to see them, and brought them back without my consent (dismissed/disregard), and I was so angry. To continue the frustration, I was eight in half months pregnant with my daughter, and while driving back we get into a car accident in the snow in Tahoe.

When we were on the dark roads, something prompted me to ask for one of my pillows from the back, and I put it on my lap, and a few moments after, someone had side swiped us, and while it was on my side, I suffered no injuries but everyone else in the car did. When we returned back home, everyone was concerned about their cuts and bruises, and wanted to be babied but I had a baby to deliver in the next two weeks and felt so angry and almost as if the gesture done by my husband was on purpose.

I was rushed at the hospital to get home because my then husband could not handle the two daughters he brought to our house without my consent and knowledge, and now wanted me to divert my energies from my first born to tend to them.

Much tension, and my first real contemplation about how I could get out of this marriage, and not suffer too much, be alive do it quick. This all happened in 2006, and a separation would not occur until December 2008.

Change Your Life Reflection Moment

Now that you have read about *The Wedding and At Home?* This was a pivotal time in my life, and I didn't realize until after I got involved that some of my hesitation was because I never wanted to be married, and was not prepared for giving up running around the country doing what I loved to do. I especially did not want my "bigger than life" attitude and being to reflect such a non-joyous occasion as my wedding day. But I had to move forward which was apart of growth.

What is it that was big in your life that caused you to be suspended in time? For me it was a wedding which is a life changing event, and decision, but what was yours? A baby out of wedlock, a job that you work 95 hours a week, but receive 40 hours of pay... Something is out of order?

Here are a few thoughts to ponder?

1. Are you making decisions that require a no, but you are adding a YES to them?
2. Have you learned the importance of waiting until you have God's full peace with all that you are doing?
3. Do you know yourself enough to know that something is just not right?
4. Have you reconciled the breach made against your soul, and done the work to repair trust for yourself?

Maybe you have felt dismissed, disregarded, and even flat out ignored, but the power is not in staying there, the ability to Love Your Start Over, is to see that level of rejection as the proper fuel for your success. There are no victims when you are determine to be a victorious person in your life.

Chapter Five

Ignoring The Real Truth, Living a Real Lie

Most people know the difference between a truth and a lie, and when it is not corrected it is distorted and becomes our reality. Here I was married, with a child, in a house that was not a home, started new business ventures to occupy my mind and time, and yet feeling very much the fraud and the lie, because I was so unhappy.

Everything about my life at that time was so not true. I was called by God to speak, live and be the model he called but I couldn't figure out how to walk away from what really was starting to become a major issue and threat to my well being.

Truth invades the soul at a time when you no longer have room for lies. I had already passed that point, but I couldn't bring myself to let others into my little world. There were some friends of mine who knew what was happening, but only to a certain extent.

The real truth was that I was afraid for my life, and trying to masquerade the reality hoping to find some answers to fix something that was falling apart fast and quick. I was not working, only doing consulting work from my firm, and my biggest contract was my husbands company. That was just all bad. I got so involved helping to build his empire that I forgot what I was doing with my own.

A *truth* is the true or actual state of a matter, and during this time, it was not. Because of several deals gone bad, we were losing $90k a month and while he was trying to stop the bleeding tending to our household bills and priorities last, we were drowning in debt and everything else.

The real lie was that I was no where near happy as I seemed, or smiled, and resented the fact that there was not a place that I could go without being judged or told, "I told you so". I just needed some help with some real issues that was stunting my personal, professional and spiritual growth.

It was in these times that I started to take a deeper look within and prepared my heart and mind for what was soon to come but I still held more to the lie rather than the truth. I was preparing to do something in my mind but actually doing it is something very different.

When you lie to yourself, you also fall into a place of betrayal and self deception. Both are harmful to your inner spirit and crushes your self worth. God has indeed made us to be free, but when we don't adequately live out our truth, even if that means that you are in a shelter, then we forfeit the rights to "our real lives".

As you finish up this chapter I admonish you to breathe, and think about the things that are holding you hostage, preventing you from living a life outside the BACKDROP realm. You must come into the forefront of your own life, and that requires dropping the curtain of fake and façade, and living up to whatever you have coming your way.

Change Your Life Reflection Moment

Now that you have read about *Ignoring The REAL Truth, Living a Real Lie?* I am sure that sometime in your process of having to start over, you felt like a fraud, a cheat, or maybe you didn't. I did because I was always in front of people, and what I was presenting was true, but the package of how they were getting it was a shell.

Your life's reflection maybe that today you are ignoring the REAL truth about your love life, your weight, your habits, your procrastination or your moving forward. Whatever it is, the lie currently has more power than the truth. Lies can't be corrected until the truth is exposed, and there is healing from the deception of not being upfront.

1. What are you LYING to yourself about?
2. Who are you LYING to, and when are they going to become important enough for you to tell them the truth?
3. Are you ready to sit in your own chair of healing?

SECTION TWO-*Living To Tell, Dying To Live*

We all have stories that we want to tell, but because we are too busy trying to live, sometimes we never get around to it. In this section you will understand the reality of my story of feeling stuck, trapped, and very angry at myself, which was the last person that I forgave in this process. This section gives you an understanding about your life story and why you must have the courage to leave, or the power to share.

While I was living to tell someone anything, I felt like I was dying to live that moment of truth and clarity. We all at some point can identify those times in our lives, when it was clear and truth was abiding. Every step we took it was in proper order, and then something happened.

For me, I saw myself replaying the story over in my head, as if I was prepping for a keynote address, indicating that I was too eager to share but not eager enough to actual do all the proper steps necessary to get my soul free. I quickly learned that this whole process had very little to do with anyone else involved. This process would be on my shoulders, and my shoulders only. I had to be willing to live, so that I could tell someone, and choose to die another day in time.

This section gives way to my *Courage To Leave*, but the battle of my mind with being *Despondent, Discouraged and Depressed*. These things showed up when I realized the *The Reality of Divorce and Separation* and the sheer fact that *I Just Don't Love This*.

The words are raw, moving and intentional to cause you to think about your own process, and the necessary steps you need to make in order to LIVE.

The power of life and death is still in the tongue of its owner: YOU!

Chapter Six

The Courage To Leave: **The Pivotal Point**

December 2007

At this time everything is strained in my marriage and in my life and I am now sleeping in the mother in law suite downstairs, where I could virtually not have to see anyone. I felt like a woman being held hostage against her will.

I was no longer having sex with my husband at this time, which only created more arguments as he thought that I was messing around with someone, but after he kept accusing me I started to think, that maybe it is him that is messing around with someone.

I made up in my mind I was leaving, with or without anything. Now we lived in this 6000 square foot home that we had already fallen behind on the payments, and he is working to try and reverse the charges or something, but I just knew that everything was crashing down and I no longer felt safe, secure or sane.

We were barely speaking and trying to "keep up the look", but then I no longer cared, and that's when he knew I was serious. I no longer argued, I just was okay trying to do what I needed to do.

So one night after we had guest over, he said we needed to talk. We did, and he says, come sleep in the bed, our bed, not down stairs, and I just told him I did not want to, it was no longer my bed, my home, and I just wasn't his wife.

Some more conversation happened, and he said well if this is the way that it is going to be, well let's have sex one more time.

And be done with it. I didn't want to because the interest was no longer there, but physically I wanted to and I liked the sound that he understood and we were over. So I said, only if you wear a condom. He said sure, but something didn't add up. His willingness should have been a clue that something was not right.

We started having sex, and everything was fine, until, midway, he takes the condom off, and just like that I am no longer sexually aroused, and I knew that I was pregnant just like that and that he did it on purpose.

I pushed him off, we started arguing, and that was the last time I had sex with him for a very long time, and the night that my son was conceived. A couple of months later, it would be verified, that I indeed was pregnant and while it might not be the most conventional thing to do, I made the decision to not involve him, down to not even telling him for months. I did not want him involved, no doctors visits nothing.

The Year 2008

While he seemed to never be around, or able to come to the doctors appointment, I was happy because that would mean I could do them without him, and move on forward. I was determined to carry him differently than I did my first child.

I called my mother and told her that I was pregnant and started crying over the phone, and she said, "Kita stop crying. I feel your pain, and it is making me hurt inside. I hate that you have had to endure this, but you will get through this. So you have two kids, the blessing is you have the Lord, your educated, and I will be here to help. You will come out of this. You just have to make a decision whether you are going to stay, and if you are you can't be looking back; or you are going to leave, and then stay away."

I thanked my mom and she prayed for me, and I curled up on the bed, and went to sleep. I slept so good, like I hadn't slept in months. Probably because I hadn't slept in months and really needed the sleep.

While still coming to grips that my life was slowly becoming like "regular people", I was starting to feel the numbing affect of being verbally talked down to, even though I was fighting back verbally, I just hadn't planned to live my life that way, so I was hanging on by an emotional thread. There is nothing wrong with "normal people" who go to work, come home, their life be consumed by family issues and stuff, I just didn't want to be regular.

My prayer life was now only in existence as a cry for help rather than a mutual relationship where the conversation is reciprocal, loving, and ongoing. This was a stop and go at best, and reading the word was every now and then.

As I got bigger and was having some difficulties in my pregnancy, my then husband begged me to come back to the bed upstairs so that I would be comfortable, but I told him I was fine, and he put the guilt trip of saying, "at least lets have some resemblance of being a family. I did, and kept all of my clothes downstairs because my heart was broken, and my mind made up it is over.

The real fight and courage to leave is dealing with the trauma while you are in it, and the aftermath of that trauma. So as I scurried around the house, trying to get situated, and protect my daughter from being involved in all of the drama, it had taken it's toll on me. In July 2008, I was laid off of my job, and I felt like I really needed that job, and although it was not a bad laying off, it felt bad, as did everything else in my life at that time.

You have to know that all of this was going on while I was doing a local and national program for women, writing two books, started a franchised gym, and a host of other things. The stress increased because I was denied unemployment, but my doctor had put me on disability because of all the stress on me so I was still able to get some income for a few weeks.

I moved back to our house in Antioch by myself and with my daughter Cayla. I then turned it into my business house, called the CYL house, had it redecorated, and it was beautiful. He said he found a way to keep the Brentwood house, so I was good. Except later he was trying to get me to get out of the house, and sell it, so he could stay in the million dollar one, or worst, get another one, without me, or use it to hold it over my head. I didn't budge, which proved to be a life saver for everyone involved in the household.

We lost the Brentwood house, and now he has nowhere to go, so he moves back into the Antioch house, and one of his daughters come with him as the other daughter decided she wanted to go live back with her mom in another State.

While there, it was not too bad, because I was focusing on me, and the baby, and made that my priority, while trying to do speaking engagement, behavioral consultant work and anything else I could do to get money to pay for water, PGE, food and everything else, since stuff was getting cut off frequently and the house that we were in was in foreclosure.

To stay focus on the task at hand, which was having a healthy baby boy, I tried to focus on what I would do once he got here. Then the hospital called, two days before I am to go in for the C-Section and tells me that the insurance company has not authorized the delivery birth and that I don't have any insurance on record. I was like oh Lord. I called the insurance company, and the first person I talked to was unwilling to help so I on purpose said thank you, while I was hanging up in her face.

I called the insurance company back, and this person said, if you can post a check today then it can reinstate the policy which had just lapsed over the last 5 days.

I did post a check, and the next day, which is the planned delivery date the hospital still did not have the ok from the insurance company for me to give birth to my son and this totally freaked me out.

The time was 9:15am, and I was scheduled to be there by 12pm for pre-op, and delivery at 2pm.

I am praying and saying God help me please, and I am crying and just saying what a serious predicament I have gotten myself into while I am crying about an 1 hour in a half later, I receive a call from the hospital that everything is fine, and the insurance cleared. I tell my husband and we get going, but by this time it is close to 11:30am and he decides to go to the cell phone company. What?

I begged him to drop me off at the hospital, but he wouldn't. So I called the hospital to tell them, I was running late and they said that they might have to reschedule. So I get out of the car, go into the store, and tell him let's go.

We get there and it is 12:15pm, and we are late. I am starting to cry inwardly because I see that this has been my life for the last 4 years. But our friends Jack and Tammy (not real names) was there at the hospital for moral support, and Tammy being a registered nurse goes up to the nurses station stalks to them and some how they take me even though now it is 12:40pm.

I made the decision that I was going to try and stay for 7 days. Got the epidural shot, had to hold onto the nurse to get it, and then came time for the baby. He came, and I let out a serious cry, while I looked at him. But there was a problem, after 6 hours, I still could not feel my legs and that was not normal.

Not only was the feeling in my leg not coming back, people weren't coming by to see me in the hospital. I then found out that my husband had forbid people to come and see me in the hospital. That was one of the many things he would say, during the pregnancy. "There won't be all those people coming in on my son". But some people ignored him because they were concerned about me.

I stayed in the hospital 6 days, and was pushed everyday to come home earlier by my husband, but because the doctor suggested that I stay longer to ensure that all was well since I remained numb in my legs longer than expected, he obliged. After spending two nights in the hospital he decided that he wanted to go and sleep in our bed at home, and I told him that was just fine. In my mind, I needed time anyways.

As I lay there in the night at the hospitals, filled with so much promise, but deathly unsure of what is to happen next. Faced with insurmountable bills, two children, in an abusive marriage, and lacking the confidence to do any work, because he embarrassed me at my job, and I thought that all jobs knew. I was needing serious help.

Got home and because we were behind on every bill, I was somewhat uneasy, but I pressed through. I started calling all of the creditors, and told them the situation and asked what kind of time would they give us to pay the bills. God showed mercy and allowed them to give me favor, stretching bills out they never should have been stretched.

Since I thought that this would be the best time for me to have an internal renewal of my faith, and turn the corner on my life as I knew it I begin to intentionally pray (setting up times), and reading the Bible. I started reading scriptures to the baby, starting getting more involved in my physical and spiritual well being, and feeling better, even though everything remained the same. But I was at least hopeful, which was a great start, since I had lost the hope of my life getting back to normal.

Then one terrible day on December 18, 2008, not even 2 months from the birth of my son, and a full 4 years, since I initially really contemplated leaving, I was involved in a heated discussion with my then husband. I was trying to stop him from man handling his teenage daughter, grabbing her and throwing her against the wall, and so I stepped in.

He was hollering and screaming, and I kept saying, just leave her be, don't talk to her until you can think a little more clearer about the situation.

He grabbed me, pinned me up against the wall, grabbed my laptop throw it on the floor with the intent to damage it, and said, "go ahead call the police, and I am going to tell them that you hit me first". Oh my God, what was I going to do? This stuff I am in, just got crazier. Even though I knew that it was not the truth, real fear came in my heart, because I remembered the time, we had an argument with some young people there, and he throw all of my business cards downstairs, by the time the police came (2 minutes), he had cleaned up the entire mess, was calm, and said Officer to what do I owe this visit.

I believed that if a man is unafraid of jumping on a police officer (which was one of the offenses he had in his previous life before me), surely I didn't stand a chance. So needless to say I am afraid, and need to just get out of there.

He told me that I could go, but I wasn't taking his children with me, and I had enough and scream, "back off of me", and that is when he grabbed me, and pinned me up on the wall. He started saying, "yeah, yeah, what are you going to do now"? But he was not talking to me. He had blacked out so quick I could tell it was someone else.

So I grabbed my phone and attempted to call the cops and he became enraged, and grabbed the phone trying to destroy it, and I got it back and ran upstairs where my son was sleeping and Cayla was lying down on the bed. I called my friend, and told her I had to get out, what happened, and could she come and pick me up. I grabbed some clothes, I don't even remember if I had shoes on my feet, and scurried out of the door with the babies, and loaded a few things in the car.

I called the cops to let them know and stated that I would need to go back and pick up my stuff, and was just shaking all over. He didn't try to stop me from leaving because I think he thought I would come back, as I had previously, but it was never to this point.

My friend and her daughter did everything to help console me, and make this very painful transition. I had no money, no job, and scared. I was crying and trying to keep my children from knowing what was going on, arrived at her house, and emotionally collapsed.

I did go back the next day, to pick up almost everything I could and pack it away some in storage and other stuff in the one room I would share with my kids for the next 4.5 months.

It was at her house that I would realize the risk, and the price of pride, ignoring the CAUTION, getting out when there was other opportunities, and taking other people's advice who indeed care. But until you want it for yourself beyond the words, you will stay and not have the courage to leave.

I couldn't help but think, how does this Certified Domestic Violence Teacher, Anger Management Trainer, Registered Marriage Family Therapist Intern, Doctorate trained student of Counseling Psychology and Social Psychology not have the ability to leave an abusive situation?

I did not understand this, especially since prior to this relationship, I had never had bad relationships with men, besides being date raped once. Now the one man I said I do to, he is crazy. Here I was an educated woman, worked hard all my life, wholesome "church girl" and I was deathly stuck in what was now a full nightmare. The prospect did not look good:

I kept rehearsing all of these in my head making it not better, but worse, because everyday I was faced with the fact that:

- had no car
- no job
- no income, denied unemployment since July 31, 2008 and now we are in December 2008
- applied for 202 jobs that I was more than qualified for and maybe two interviews and no job
- sleeping on friends couch
- overweight
- loss of confidence and value of self
- wondering where the Hell is God

This is the part that stifled me, and why I didn't leave my husband in the first place. I was trying to "cure myself" so that I didn't look so bad. But it wasn't working because as long as I was not completely "true to myself" there would be no healing, and definitely no wholeness. I needed help and I needed it fast in order for me to experience a true starting over moment.

Then I got a call from a college roommate, who told me that her organization was looking for a trainer, and the contract potential was $100K. So I did the proposal and they accepted it, but they wanted to start off with one training first for $10K, and that was fine with me because I was broke.

I did it, was excited, but I was stuck too mentally to think that I could move out on my own, and so I stayed at my friends house, until the death of my mom, and brother, and upon my return from the funerals it was of necessity that I move out.

With my stuff packed up and by the door and no place to go, literally no place to go, I called another friend, and asked if I could come to her house for a few days to a week and she said yes. I put my stuff in her garage, stayed there and then I did the unthinkable; I sat and thought too long about my situation and felt like, why should I be on people's couches, floors, and he be living in the house that he didn't even want me to keep, so I called my then husband, and said that I needed to come and stay and I was going to be in Cayla's room, and me and the two kids did that.

Hell on earth had just interrupted the atmosphere, but I wanted to be a little more comfortable than I was. So we ended up having to leave our beautiful home, which no longer had beauty which is another story in and of itself, and ended up staying at our friends recently left foreclosed million dollar home.

Grateful but utterly embarrassed because now legally we are considered squatters. We stayed there for a couple of months, and it was in that house that I made the decision, weight is coming off, and the birthing of my Walk It Off Girl came forth. This was the summer of 2009. All the while still in appeals about my unemployment, since July 31, 2008. A full year had passed.

Now with no prospects of anything, I am reinventing self. Start picking up more momentum in book sales and speaking, and secretly thinking I need to go and live in Texas with my family. But my plan was be done with the marriage, and then go.

The courage to leave is a lengthy process, and after going through what I went through I felt like I needed to send the 10,000 women that I had counseled or trained over the years, an apology as I was hell bent on them packing up their stuff and getting out of dodge. But it really is never that easy.

Silently Suffering

While being at my friends house, the one who came and got me on December 18, 2008, my mission was still about having the courage to leave permanently, but I realize very quickly that there are stages of what happens when you do make the decision to forge forward.

Most of what people go through when they take the step to remove themselves from harms way, you suffer silently. You feel guilty, angry, and sense of self is lowered because you live too low to become with.

So while I am there at my friends house, I find out in late December 2008, that my mom was not well, and that they are running test on her in Texas during her yearly trip to visit the rest of my family.

With that on my brain, I believe and assume that she is going to be okay and I try to forge forward with my own life. But she did not get better she got worse.

Having to walk with the kids because he would not give me my car, and stated that since he bought it for me, it was his, so I left it at that and continued to walk, but hatred and resentment had built up so strong. I came to the realization that leaving didn't offer me much initial consolation as my staying. I simply said, I don't care for this, and contemplated leaving my friends house and going back. Even though he didn't have anything, no income, just cars, the house, it felt like he had everything and I had nothing.

Time would go on and I started drifting into great despondency, discouragement and depression. Although I was still speaking, and doing trainings, I was slowly losing inspiration. I keep trying to show up big for myself, but I was really emotionally battered, physically overweight by 50 pounds, and psychological off. Spiritually I was not at my greatest, but I had prayer, which I believe kept me afloat for all of the other major hits, while I was trying to Start Over and Love it!

The courage to leave was big for me, but as I stated it was just the beginning. The other layers that happens when you pull away from something toxic is learning to come into your own, and try to breathe the freshness of that but when you are wrestling with *despondency, discouragement, and depression*, you are fighting for your life.

You can't hope for something that you are unwilling to actually do. Everyday I wanted something better, but I made very baby steps towards it, and the biggest one was the realization that I didn't want it bad enough to risk it all.

We would eventually move two more times, and after having to call the cops on him again, and having him arrested, and restraining order on him, the next week, I received a call from EDD stating that I won my one year in a half case, and they were going to reimburse me the money.

I was leaping for joy, was already looking for a new place, and then my then husband asked if he could help me move into the new place. I thinking that he just wanted to help said sure, and he moved in with me and the kids. I knew that it was the end when we started, but he vowed to make it work. We went to counseling, and things panned out until I said that he was going to have to pay for some of the bills, and the anger and violent verbal outburst started, but this time, I had enough.

I slept in the living room for the duration of my time there, and needed to move again, and the places that I wanted was not ready and too expensive for the amount of money that I had, but I knew that this was it. He moved out into a house that I did not believe was his, and I asked him to take the kids for a week while I figured out what I would do. This time would allow me time to fast and pray and really look for a job.

So while at a One Stop Center, a woman that works there, ask me who I am, and rather than have a long story of "the impressive me", I said, someone looking for work so that I can rebuild my own businesses. She and another lady told me about this job, and within one week, I was hired. This happened in May 2010 almost two years since my last job. Starting Over is in my view, I just don't love it.

I indeed had to leave the house that I was in, and so I told him that I was coming to stay with him (he though that I was coming back), but I was not.

When the time came, he let me stay at his house for 3 months month, and one night I woke up at 3am, in December, and my SOUL said enough, got online went to Craigslist, and made notes about where I was calling, and I was going to move out. I was working for the County, and the time is now. He awoke to find me up, and asked me, what I was doing? I told him, "looking for housing". He said, "oh are you looking for a place for all of us?" I said, "no", and while he tried to go off, like a parent ignores the temper tantrum of a child, I ignored it, and he soon stopped, and stormed outside at 4:45am.

Found a place and told them my TRUE story, but that I needed to Start Over again, and that couple gave me the opportunity to stay in a lovely 2 bedroom, 1.5 bathroom, upstairs/downstairs condo, in a great community. And it was mine. Another starting over moment was happening, and while I liked it, I hadn't fell in love with it yet.

Got into my new house, which was a cute little condo, upstairs down stairs, and now only thing left to do was get my car. Prayed where should I go, and then I went was excited about it, but didn't negotiate the price of the monthly properly, even thought I could pay for it, but it would be stretching me. But I got it, and told him that I don't have share the car with him, because I have my own.

Excited, feeling liberated, and definitely in the "starting over" mode. This was the beginning of something new and fresh, and I was rejoicing because of it. I had lost 50lbs and it showed, along with a new sense of living.

Change Your Life Reflection Moment

Now that you have read about *The Courage to Leave: A Pivotal Point?* I had the thought to leave, but not the courage to actually do it, and then I had to do it when physical harm came my way. I was still trying to find a way to fix things, and to make it not seem so "bad", but it was just that bad and then some. So I left, and had a lot of loss during that time.

The death of my mother on April 29, 2009, then the death of my brother on April 30, 2009, with passing of my Aunt Gwen on May 15, 2010. All three died from cancer, all three were strong, but it was all too much and I was in my lowest place. But everything during this season was pivotal for my moving forward, and pressing on towards the place that would eventually catapult me into a real starting over and truly loving it.

So maybe you have had to leave something or you need to leave something, because you have so much living to do, but your staying stuck is hampering your growth.

Take a moment and realign your thoughts in a very real way:

1. When was the last time you had the courage to do something big?
2. Is it time for another pivotal moment in your life?
3. How has suffering silently crippled your faith?
4. If fresh starts are available when do you plan on taking yours?

Chapter Seven

Despondent, Discouraged and Depressed

When you are starting over, or simply have to go into a different direction in all areas of your life, you might be met with *despondency, discouragement and depression.*

Despondency has the feel of depression but it is not. It is the state of being *despondent* or operating in a depressed spirit from loss of courage or hope. It is the feeling of total dejection, thrown away, not wanted, and it continues as our lips give it fuel with our belief.

This emotion and feeling gives way and is an open door to *discouragement*, which not only sits very strongly on you if you don't cast it down, but discouragement is the self sabotaging thinking that you do to yourself but trying to project it from coming from somewhere else.

Discouragement according to Webster's diction means to deprive of courage, hope, or confidence; dishearten; dispirit, to dissuade, to obstruct by opposition or difficulty to simply hinder.

In this stage of having the courage to leave or to start something fresh, you too, might run into despondency or discouragement, but don't allow the sadness of time loss, cause you to turn inward and it become depression.

Depression is something that I have dealt with before as a child growing up, and as a young adult. It is also the subject of one my books called, "When Believers Become Depressed, Helping Those Who Believe in God", I share the reality of depression and spiritual depression and that there are 21 symptoms that help people to identify and characterized it in those making massive changes.

Depression to me is the overwhelming feeling of negativity, where there seems to be no end, or no solution; at least the appearance of no end and because of the internal thought process of the person it is fueled by their lack of doing things.

The lack and inability to do things is the issue with depression. Coupled with loss of desire, and change in social behavior such as being around friends, family and doing activities that you love to do. Depression longs to grip the person into the constant flow of focus on the negative, while forgetting all the good things going on in the person's life.

So in your Starting Over process, you will deal with symptoms of depression, but like anything else you must put it into proper perspective. At times everybody feels bad, sad and sometimes just plain out of it, but how long and for what reason is the tell tale sign that will either help or hurt your chances of getting or remaining free.

You should know that when I was making the adjustments to move forward I was functionally depressed. While I had no time to sit, mope and just do nothing, I went forward, but my spirits were low, and I had to constantly remind myself what I was doing was right. It is never easy to go through trauma, emotional setbacks, and then redo your entire life, and way of being. It gets tough, but this is where I found solace in the Holy Spirit, and the Word of God in my tough place of living.

There is no other greater feeling than to know that while you may be feeling *despondent, discouraged, and depressed,* there is a real way out. This way requires a new way of thinking, and doing. It also requires you to be present so that the work can be done. You will not be able to get different results by using the same tools and techniques.

Habits have to be changed, and a new hope has to be given. I found that I could not do the changes in and of myself, I had to rely on God, even though it was a struggle, because I came to my own conclusion that most of what I was dealing with was a direct result of my DISOBEDIENCE to him, and while God does not hold things over your head, I had to walk out the consequences of my actions. The agony of this was more than I anticipated.

Rest assured that there were many instances of grace, mercy and long periods of being able to breathe, but I had to cling onto God's Word and trust that it would all start to make sense and work for my good.

I held on to many scriptures, and one of my favorites was **Psalm 138:8** *"The Lord will perfect that which concerneth me: thy mercy, O Lord, endureth for ever forsake not the works of thine own hands."*

And **Jeremiah 29:11,** which says, *"For I know the thoughts that I think toward you, saith the Lord, thoughts of peace and not of evil, to give you an expected end."*

Although at this time I didn't have a knowing that I would be okay, I really was stepping out there by faith to believe that it would all come together.

When our emotions get involved it triggers so many other things and makes us vulnerable to poor judgment and bad decisions. So we must be aware, look at and identify the things that are plaguing our lives. For me it was despondency, discouragement and depression, for you it may be something else. Approach, deal and confront it, head on, and watch things get clearer.

Change Your Life Reflection Moment

Now that you have read about *Despondent, Discouraged and Depressed?* It was like a heavy blanket that when I thought I was free and light, it would come back on me. I really battled, and wondered is that how I am going to go out?

I really have to deal with this too okay. But then I had to really look at the situation and decided that it was not just one event that had happen, there were several things that had taken place. Loss of self, home, job, money, family, mom, brother, aunt, health, self-respect and the list goes on.

I am so glad that somewhere in there I decided that I needed to not self-loathe, or be victimized by my situation any longer, it was time to leap forward. So it is with you, choose in your heart to leap forward and make your change from the inside first.

Right now, look at the questions below and seriously take a look at what is on you.

1. Do you have a hard time bouncing back after a traumatic situation?
2. Do you think that your mood change is normal?
3. Are you sure you know when you are depressed?
4. Maybe you aren't despondent, discouraged, or depressed, but you are _____?

Chapter Eight

The Reality of Divorce & Separation From Anything

Even though many people are walking away from their marriages, I really did want it to work. Some of the reasons was selfish (didn't want to look like a fool, or a person who went against what I knew was not right), the other reasons was because I really wanted to have this family not be broken up. But the damage was too much for my psyche, and my soul.

When divorce happens, or when you are separating from anything like a job, or career, or loss of ability to take care of self, it weighs heavily on your heart and messes with your head.

In my opinion and experience from working with marital couples for years, divorce doesn't get serious until both parties are in two separate households, and moving forward in their lives. Then the reality sets in, that this thing is over, or at least on its way to be.

Divorce requires a real look at yourself, and you will start asking the questions, what is happening to me? How do I find the road to healing? We know for those that have faith in God, that we rely on the strength of God's word to help us, but some of us, still don't get through the reality of the break.

Even if it was a union that should not have been, you have been tied to, and joined together with someone for a period of time, that creates a covenant, which is not breakable, just because you want out.

During the pivotal points in my life, I started seeking out places, that I could go where I would get the word of God, but that would be specific to my current issue of divorce, and how to help my children deal with it as well. I was blessed with resources that would help continue my healing process of the divorce. During the time my daughter was in competition cheer, the Director Debbie, told me about a Divorce Care 16 week class that was going to be starting at their church; and it was FREE. I went to the church and signed me and my kids up for the class.

Signing up for the class was the best thing that could happen to us, and it would prove to be a great place of Starting Over in a new way. We have since gone through the class twice, because for my children it serves as therapy and another opportunity to be expose to God's word to help heal any open wounds.

In the Divorce Care class we learned what the foundation of our healing is and that is a personal relationship with Jesus Christ. We also had to recognize who was at the center of our life? This was interesting, because when you are going through divorce or the separation of anything you come to realize that God is not at the center of your life, maybe in words but indeed he is somewhere around there but just not at the center.

I exalted my problems, issues, failures, traumas above God, myself, and my purpose. It was at the center, draining me of all the emotional and spiritual juice I needed to move forward. My problems essentially became my idols, my full-time job and I silently worshipped them, even though that was the thing I was trying to get free from.

If what you are separating from is not a spouse or a job, whatever it is, you will still go through some level of grief and loss while you are making sure that you are comfortable with the decision to move forward. Elisabeth Kubler Ross, started the whole concept of the 5 Stages of grief and loss. Those five stages are **Denial, Anger, Bargaining, Depression and Acceptance.**

When it became apparent that I was indeed going to have to go through with the divorce, my staying in it for a longer time than I should was apart of the denial that I had about whether or not I should leave. And when you consider the etymology of the word divorce, you will understand the difficulty.

I went through every stage of grief and loss, because it was real, and I was trying to make sense of current life's situations. No amount of stages can cause you to truly understand the impact that divorce has on your soul and spirit. Whether it was a good marriage or bad one, separation, loss and grief are all still very hard things to endure.

Divorce literally means a "judicial declaration dissolving a **marriage** in whole or in part, especially one that releases the marriage partners from all matrimonial obligations. Its any formal separation of husband and wife according to established custom and results in a total separation; disunion".

There is so much that happens when you make the decision to divorce a spouse of any length of time, but especially of 10 years being together (6.5 years of marriage). It is not just a walking away which is the real reality of divorce and separating from things, it's the WORK that is involved in it. It's the bargaining that you are trying to deal with, "can I stay", "should I have done this, that or the other?" God if only things didn't have to be this way, I would do it better. You can't bargain what is essential broken and gone.

When you step away from something, you must consider several things, and then act upon it.

1. Your timing
2. Those that are involved in your situation (ie. Children)
3. The real cost associated with your divorce or separation
4. How to not look back but stay in forward mindset
5. What is in your hand to work with?
6. Who is apart of your support network?

These questions are the beginning when you are dealing with the reality of divorce and separation of something. It is hard on the mental faculties if you keep losing things, and not replace it with renewal of mind and spirit.

Change Your Life Reflection Moment

The Reality of Divorce and Separation From Anything gives you an opportunity to consider all things, and to move with more knowledge and understanding about what you are really dealing with. For some people leaving a toxic relationship could mean their life, or a family member's life. It also causes great agony on the emotions, because you have to pick up the pieces and keep moving.

But what do you do, if everything has stopped, and you can't really keep moving. This can be such a major struggle. Trying to keep it all together, and you can't. You will have to figure out a way to not cut yourself down when you are disconnecting yourself, and separating.

Ask yourself these questions:

1. Are you willing to do the work necessary to really become divorced, or separated from a thing?
2. Are you giving yourself enough space to do the work in?
3. Are you relying on your support to do things that you should be doing?

Then do the work that is necessary to have your Starting Over Reflection moment.

Chapter Nine

I Don't Love This

So with everything that had been happening, I realized that my choices and other things that I had no control over really put me n a jam, and no amount of smiling was going to take away the real feeling that I don't like this at all, and I definitely did not love it.

Yes we are taught to be "content" in all things in the Lord but I couldn't shake the fact that I was the initiator of my own downfall and mentally that was messing with me. Everyday for more than 1 year I cried, because I didn't love this. The tearing apart, the brokenness, the pulling away, the gutting out, was all just a bit too much.

When you have allowed yourself too many times to not trust your instincts, it weakens your ability to trust yourself, and you begin to not love yourself and then the inevitable happens; you just stop caring. When your love for doing the best in your life ceases, you invite so many other things.

You will, like I did have to get back to liking the person that you were before the need for Starting Over took place. Until you love who you are, and are able in truth to walk out your journey you will not love the process, and it will feel more difficult to get through.

And please don't fool yourself, because "saying it doesn't mean you believe it". There are seasons, periods, and times that some things in your life just might not work, but when I saw almost everything not working, I attributed it to being something wrong with me.

This initially made me look at my process harshly and feeling out of sorts, creating more emotional withdrawals and causing me to stay longer in a situation that I just wanted to run out of. It wasn't me, and it was not what I was purposed for, but I could not relinquish the posture of staying in place.

As I grew in faith, and in trust that I was indeed going to get my life back, I begin to like where I was, and then when I started to smile, worship and praise where the heartache remained, I then begin to change my view, and as you will read in the last section of this book, you will realize the importance of getting your mind, spirit, body and soul back in order and in full alignment with God's word over your life.

The one thing I know for sure is that we can not pretend to be doing anything when nothing is actually being done. I was telling my friends, boldly and courageously "I am so done with this, so out of here, and I don't care what happens, I should have done this years ago".... But to actually execute that which I spoke was different. This is the main reason why I didn't love the process, because I wasn't doing all the steps.

Change Your Life Reflection Moment

Maybe you have identified with the *I Don't Love This* chapter, and although it was intentionally short to give you time to actually think about and write and journal your experience of how you don't like the things going on in your starting over process.

Until we come to grips with where we are on the emotional scale of our soul we will forever be fooling ourselves into thinking that things are going to change, and that we are going to enjoy the experience.

Here are a few things to keep in mind, when you are in the midst of your "I Don't Like This" stage. While it is a very natural feeling, and you will encounter this, God's grace will sustain you through the hard times of the mental flip flops that happen. You just have to hang on until the end.

1. Are you beating up on yourself more than you should?
2. Do you really know how bad the situation is?
3. Write out what is good in your current life versus the bad thing that is going on. What are your learning because of it?

SECTION THREE- *Starting Over, Letting Go and Loving It*

Strength From Within: The Power To Start Again

Everyone in my opinion has that something inside of them that gives them a sense of hope, and determination. Even those who have suffered severe trauma and abuse is able to grasp the tangible effects of believing in the power to bounce back from terrible situations.

While there are instances where peoples environmental structures and circumstances will not allow them to draw strength from within, I believe that every person is given the opportunity to choose to call upon another strength: God

This book was written in hopes to create a social awareness that strength comes from within, and yes you can start again. It is my utmost desire that the candid conversations, personal experiences, psychological explanations, and spiritual revelations that start you on a lifetime journey of self recovery, one that is rooted in self love you have been able to experience some of it through the first two sections of the book.

I spent time giving you some of the backdrop, and inside mindset of who, what, when, where and how, and now I want to spend the remaining time sharing with you the joy of starting over and that when you understand that your strength comes from God and His word, you will find your restoration in full effect.

We are living in challenging times, but where there is a challenge there is a reward. I believe these are good times as well, strengthening and building us up to be better people, mothers, fathers, workers, and essentially anything that we are trying to be.

Our perspectives will takes us a long way, but it is the place in which you draw strength from that will determine your output. There are many resources, references, and ideologies that you can adopt and take on, and there would be nothing wrong with it, but I encourage you to broaden your thoughts and step into a great place of starting fresh.

Just because you start fresh, doesn't mean you start from scratch. I had to learn this truth, and decide that I would use some of the things that I was doing previously and be willing to let go of what did not fit in this moment in time.

It was amazing to see how much lighter my load felt, not to mention how quickly I seemed to learn some things, grow in some areas and starting feeling both healed and whole.

Take it upon your self the next few pages, and be introduced to what you know is the beginning of something that will last a lifetime. I have decided to make the last section flow in a little different way, so that you can feel every word, and let it arise in your spirit so that you not only read it, but it gets formed in you.

May the next section and pages be intriguing enough to stir up your conscious mind, and may all questions be answered as you seek for God's inspiring and intelligent voice to sound the alarm of wholeness in your soul. You were designed to be free in Christ, and He has given us the power to overcome all things.

Walk out your God given destiny and uphold the biblical truth that with God all things are possible to them that believe. So believe with your heart and not with your head, and gain strength from within, where Christ dwells richly, letting go all that is old, and non useful, and gaining a new perspective and understanding of that which is new.

You were made with the ability to have Victory in front of your name, and even if you are hurting in pain today, albeit physical, emotional, spiritual or psychological, I pray complete wholeness over your entire being, and I speak to the beginning of who you were prior to the devastation. Even if the devastation was caused by your choices, that is why He died, so that grace, his grace would trump our poor and sometimes disobedient ways and decision.

You can make it, you will be able to start afresh!

Chapter Ten

The Mental Climb Back

Mentally when you are starting over, and needing to get a different way of thinking and living, it seems like an endless journey of constant ups and down. Your mind drifts, your flesh is totally weak and your spirit is drained. You look, you search and you desperately hope for that word, or thing that will give you the ump that you know you have lost.

In my Starting Over, the mental fight was the worst as this is one of the things that the enemy tries to use against me. You have heard it be said before that whatever it is you are called to usually is the thing that was a problem for you.

For the last 16 years, I have had the distinct privilege of working with children and adults ages 2 and up, with a variety of different things going on. Some were diagnosed as depressed, manic, histrionic, bipolar, and some even schizophrenia.

When working with these clients, I realized that if they are dealing with this and on medication, then surely I can overcome what I am walking through. Even though I sometimes saw IMPOSSIBILITY written over it.

I added this chapter and put it in this section, because I wanted this chapter to be more about how you make the comeback mentally. What do you need to do to ensure that you are climbing upward and not into a downward way. And how important it is to be in a renewed mindset, one that is willing to let go of the old, and recondition yourself for the new.

Like anything, there has to be a beginning. So wherever you may be mentally at this time, whether you are at the beginning, the middle or the end of Starting Over, you will have to pace your thinking, and calm down. You can not operate like you did when all was going well, but you can not create the demise for yourself.

During the worst times of my life and when I felt like I could see the rainbow, one thing was constant and that was PRAYER. Now I will be truthful, sometimes it was filled with ranting, and venting, and worrying, but when I would say soul you need God, and you can not keep holding on to stuff in the manner in which you do; I felt a break.

It is important to note that God will send many people your way to help you navigate through your journey and climb, but you will have to be open to know that they were sent by him, and the impact of them coming will not add to your harm, but will be very much your help.

There were several key people who was strategic in my mental climb back, great friends, people that I did not know personally, but because I heard them say a word, or I read their book it boosted my belief in self. You have to put your foot on the bottom step, and only look to thank God for the ability to climb. Cast off doubt, insecurity, shame, pride, and the feeling of WHY, and just climb.

Your climb mentally is just as significant as your courage to leave. I found out as you probably have found out that our minds is what keeps reminding us, and making us punish ourselves for decisions that we made. But your mind, is apart of you, and you control your mind.

Because of the level of trauma you experienced it greatly impacts the mind, and it is the most difficult at times to convince to go back to a place of normality and wholeness. This was really my main thought when I wrote this is helping people to look at the impact of trauma on the mind which can be the most devastating, even worst then the actual trauma itself.

Traumatic events can leave us feeling unsafe. They disrupt our beliefs and assumptions about the world. Our sense of ability to control our life can be shattered. I know that I questioned my value, my ability, my knowledge, and even my gifts. When making the mental climb back you may question how much influence you have over your life and your life choices and it may cause you not to trust yourself.

While the mind is filled with its conscious and subconscious parts, you are still the authority over it, and what you introduce to it is key to what remains. Your ears also play a major role in your mind being renewed. All parts of the body, work in tandem together. If something is out of place, then it impacts the other parts, so your mind must come back, better and stronger.

To help you as you read further, I want you to remember to ask yourself these things:

1. Mentally where are you? (Flighty, numb, alert, hypersensitive)
2. What tools have you been using thus far in your mental climb back?

Your mind is the gateway to your most intimate parts, and if it is clouded with regrets, unforgiveness of self or others, climbing will be tough, or shall I say tougher. Even during this climb back, don't inundate yourself with "so much POSITIVE" stuff which I know is very contrary to what you have heard, but I have seen its negative affects in me, and in many that I have counseled.

When you are dealing with your own negative, simply reading all positive stuff does not necessarily have an immediate positive impact on you. Sometimes it causes you to start over analyzing yourself, and sometimes you become worse, because you are measuring and comparing yourselves to something else or someone else.

For those of you who may be numb, and unable to catch your natural breathe, I stop in the middle of the writing this book, and I say to you, LIVE, may the breathe of God blow on you even right now.

I know that this is just a book, but some people it will be the catalyst to their coming out of a lot of mental and emotional darkness.

There is power in words, especially those that are charged by God. So with that, this is what I continue to say to the numbed person,

"I command your soul to feel again. There will be no numbing out when you need to feel the hurt, heal, and get whole."

You will be able to go deeper in the Starting Over and Loving It Workbook that is designed to help you totally get rid of the fear and anxiety of actually completing what you started and even attempting to make the mental journey back.

This Starting Over business is much more than leaving, describing, or even surviving your story. You have to know that indeed it all was for your good, and for that alone, it is going to be okay.

There is a deep desire for every human to come to the place of resolve concerning their life's purpose, destiny, and reason why you are living? Give your soul a break and let your mind be free in knowing that there is power in God, his Word, and the leading of the Holy Spirit and decide that you need to make the necessary changes, and grace will be waiting for you.

Chapter Eleven

Stress, Physical Fatigue and Sickness
"If your soul is sick so is your whole body"

During the last 5 years of being married, I was 50 pounds over weight, partially I am to blame for this, I couldn't shake what was like a cold, but had the affects of allergies, and I had problems with my bowels (irritable bowel syndrome), and I was sluggish to say the least.

When you have a lot of stress, and trauma, you will have something physical go on in your body and you will probably be sick more times than you should. When you have experience stress you will notice the changes that it has to your body, such as dizziness, shortness of breath, racing heart, shaking, feeling hot, flushed, and sweating.

You can see the effects of these changes to the body in many of the symptoms of stress, such as racing heart, dizziness, nausea, shortness of breath, shaking, feeling hot and flushed, and sweating. These symptoms work so that you don't miss the cues, and end up dead or stroked out. Your body sends warning, but if you have not be paying attention, stroke will seem to sneak up on you.

As we change and have many experiences throughout life, our beliefs and assumptions typically evolve over time. With stress and trauma those beliefs that we use to make sense of the world around us change almost automatically.

In any loss it is common to experience a wide range of psychological symptoms, including intrusive thoughts, worry, difficulty sleeping, trouble focusing or concentration, bouts of crying, blame or self-judgment and lack of satisfaction, but when it dominates your life, and erodes your thought process, then we have another issue.

When you have multiple traumas or have been repeatedly exposed to life-threatening events can fatally impact your mind and body. Parts of the brain become de-sensitized, where you don't feel the kind of flight or fight sensory that you should; or you stay on high alert and perceive threats all around all the time, leaving you jumpy and anxious.

When you have anxiety your brain and body are always moving, fighting which is why you are fatigue physically. These things are detriment to body especially if you have insomnia on top of everything else. Ultimately when you are stressed, and physically fatigued, you will get sick.

Your immune system is not designed for the constant shocks that it keeps taking, of starting up and shutting down, fighting off foreign agents, and all the other stuff going on in your body ALL at the same time. If your body and mind are not in alignment with one another it makes the whole body sick.

All body parts need to be in working condition for optimal functioning and to be at your best. Even though during the dismal times in my life, I was relying on God to help me, there was some things that he required of me; take care of my body, the temple. I was required to renew my mind by using the word of God. I also had to have faith and to hope in his word. As I was required to do this so are all of you who say you will trust God with your life.

Special Prayer:

God I am agreeing with the reader of this book that if they are suffering from stress controlled, or uncontrollable, fatigue, and constant sickness, that something would break in their mind, in their spirit, that would give them freedom and a time of healing and wholeness.

I pray that your spirit would direct them to properly plan all things, and for them to seek after you regarding all things. Father you sent your word and healed them. I thank you for your word and it's power to transform lives. In Jesus name, amen.

Chapter Twelve

Spiritual Momentum

"Not as though I had already attained, either were already perfect: but I follow after if that I may apprehend that for which also I am apprehended of Christ Jesus….but this one thing I do, forgetting those things which are behind, and reaching forth unto those things which are before. I press toward the mark for the prize of the high calling of God in Christ Jesus"- *Philippians 3:12-14*

Spiritual Momentum is a necessary component when Starting Over. I credit the above verse in Philippians as being one of the major pivotal thrusts that I had when it was time to gain traction and move from one mental, physical, emotional and spiritual dimension to another.

Momentum is the force or speed of **movement**; as of a physical **object** or course of events. It is the driving power and strength behind a thing. It is the thing that gets you moving, and is sustained by the force of that thing. So when you have spiritual momentum, you have to know what is the force behind the course of events.

For me, Philippians 3:12-15 really spoke to me and helped to propel me into a place of mental and spiritual determination to follow after the plan of God for all of my needs and wants. To know that you have a past is one thing, but to keep being reenergized by your past, is something total different.

Your spiritual momentum will always start in prayer, with acknowledging your personal truth to the only wise God, who I believe is our creator. He sees the beginning from the end, but gives us opportunity to be apart of the process.

Prayer is dialogue between you and God, and is fortified by truth, honesty, and belief that God can hear you and answer you. Prayer is essential in building spiritual momentum, and maintaining it.

Prayer is the life line that kept me focused and at least present, while I was going from place to place mentally and spiritually. Your ability to trust that a God you can not see, He will make Himself known to you, if you can but pray by faith, believing that He is more than able to hear and deliver you out of all your distresses.

So to jump start your spiritual momentum, you must pray. Take time and confess to God what you know is true about you, repent, be sorrowful for whatever, so that your heart is FREE to receive all that He has in store for you.

Spiritual Momentum then moves from prayer, to reading God's word, and other things that move your spirit man. So let's look at the one I deemed the most important: God's Word.

First of all even those that are not "practicing Christians" read the bible, and take the biblical truths, apply them, so that they see the word working for them. We too, who say that we are apart of Him must take some time and read biblical truth which I believe will help digest the truth of your situation.

God told me that His grace trumps my poor decisions, so to the point where nothing else will even seem to matter. I know for a certainty, that God will cause you to thrive in the midst of what seems like a dead situation just because the spirit of truth and grace is attached to it.

This is why I took to the scripture Philippians 3:12-15 and really begin to live by it.

The verse says,

> *"Not as though I had already attained, either were already perfect: but I follow after if that I may apprehend that for which also I am apprehended of Christ Jesus....but this one thing I do, forgetting those things which are behind, and reaching forth unto those things which are before. I press toward the mark for the prize of the high calling of God in Christ Jesus. Let us therefore, as many as be perfect, be thus minded: and if in any thing ye be otherwise minded, God shall reveal even this unto you."*.

So through all the time that I was groaning and complaining, and trying to press through the difficulty, heart wrenching stuff, essentially this verse let me know GIRL you are looking to much at the past, holding onto it for dear life, and forgetting what is in front of you.

When the truth of these verses hit my soul, I cried out to God, Lord, it is stated (because I am now in somewhat of a disbelieving place) that I am created after your image, and I know that you don't hate yourself, so I need a make over in my mental and spiritual status. As I continued to pray, and read then the motion and force behind my movements got greater.

I was now in spiritual momentum mode. I had the desire to not keep looking back, because His presence in prayer was reminding me that there was so much in front of me.

After prayer, reading his word, and other things that would spiritually lift me, or intellectually stimulate me God said, now you have to retrain your flesh to adhere to the spirit and not to the dictates of your own murmuring and complaining. So I had to include fasting. This takes your spiritual momentum to a whole other level, and really is a book within itself.

What I can say about fasting, is that it didn't just cause me not to eat certain things during certain times, it prepared me to get in the mode of coming to God, without the weight and distractions of everything else. It created a place of discipline where I had lost it. It gave resemblance of order, authority and humility. Fasting catapulted me back into a place of consecration (setting me apart so I can focus) and preparing me for the work that he called me to do in spite of life's challenges.

Your spiritual momentum will happen, when you use God's Word, Give Up Your Will and Heed to His way. It is a tough choice to make but I haven't found anyone who wasn't really glad they made it.

So your thriving begins with your submitting, and your desire to have more of God's peace, and joy. He said that he wants you to have life and that more abundantly, but I suspect that we have to quit measuring up with his abundant life is versus our own.

Regaining Self-Respect

When you stay in the realm of having spiritual momentum, and you are looking at yourself differently, you will begin to feel the full restoration of self-respect.

Often when we make poor decisions it blurs our thoughts and tries to permanently affect our egos, and if they are fragile, then we begin to lose confidence in self, and start to speak ill of ourselves. When you have made the conscious HEART decision that I will not let that which I have ENDURED (overcome) cause me to denigrate myself, and not value my worth.

Self-respect is probably one of the last things that a battered man or woman gains back, because of all the shame that was attached to the process of your trial. I can vividly remember when I started to gain self-respect, and that was the day that I decided I need to no longer carry 195 pounds on a 5'4" body frame.

When I made the choice to get my body back, and stuck to my plan of not letting anything disturb my practice of walking everyday (sometimes up to 2.5 hours) or my peace of knowing that this is not the end: I then found my self-respect.

When we use things like food, sex, titles, spirituality, education, gifts, talents, we only hide from the truth of where we are. I had no idea that I had that much of an intense love affair with food. So when you can look at yourself in the mirror however you see it, and declare I can no longer, and I will no longer be this way, then self-respect will start to envelope.

To respect yourself is to love yourself beyond the state that you currently see yourself in. You have to breathe it. Start with getting up and jumping out of bed, and say, "I thank God for waking me up today". Put on some music that will make you move. And remind yourself, this too shall pass.

Chapter Thirteen

Gaining Godly Contentment
"Godliness with contentment is great gain"- *Timothy 6:6*

When I begin to love the process of starting over, I had to gain contentment and make sure that God was in it. When I interviewed a Christian CEO of a Billion Dollar Company, I asked him what advice would he give someone like me who is Starting Over, who has made the decision to follow the full path of what God has called me to do, but I really want to leave a legacy? His response,

> *"Don't measure yourself by man's standards. Measure it only by Gods. When you measure yourself by man's standards, you will come up with something totally different from what God desires, and you will not be effective nor will you be happy".*

From his statement I got that the world, which includes the men and women in it *measure* one another by their own standards, but God *equates* people to HIS. So I decide to look up the words measure and equate, and found it to be very interesting.

To *measure* means have a unit or standard of **measurement**. It's a system by which an instrument, gives the extent, dimensions, quantity, of something, determining it's value while it is compared to something else. To *equate* means to regard, treat, or represent as equivalent. It also implies to reduce to an average; make correction or allowance and create it's own standard of comparison.

So as I stopped measuring myself to all these rules that I learned all of these years, I could see how God saw me in His eyes, and then acted accordingly. If you are going to have godly contentment, you will have to remove the factor of man's standard and equate your life to God's plan. It is so much bigger than what you or anyone else could think of.

Your joy, peace and happiness is not in the arms, or mouth of another person, it is simply in the godly expression and inspiring word of God over your life.

I have seen as I too have spent many years distracted by the thoughts of other people, and their purposeful yet untimely flattering words that only caused me to seek for more approval and validation rather than have the boldness and courage to live out the full counsel of God's word over my life.

Starting over is not the literal place of going back to the beginning, but in a figurative sense you must go back to the place where you laid down you're your contentment in this world, and finish the race you started. If by chance you have been running someone else's race, then starting over, is appropriate for you.

We can only be responsible for the race that has our name on it, and until you seek God, the author and finisher of your faith, you will not know which race you are in.

It is not enough to just want to be a "good person', do random acts of kindness, but unknowingly pervert the truth to match your life. When God is in the picture, as I have stated in my book, *God IS The Business....And He Wants Everyone Employed*, I suggest that God is about 5 things: **People, Life, Love, Truth and Change.** Since he is having godly contentment helps you to see him in all of these ways.

You can start over, and you can be content, even if you are starting at the bottom. If you keep going in the race with your name on it, you will cross the finish line at the designated time designed for you to finish, but there can be no looking back.

Loving The Skin Your In
"To love oneself is a form of true satisfaction with everyone else"

Yeah, finally after 4 long arduous years, I can say it loud and clear, I LOVE THE SKIN I AM IN. This is an important aspect in your Starting Over journey. You have to love the skin your in, and not give excuses to the SIN that you may be in.

If you are overeating, that is a sin against your body and it is called gluttony. Truly that is not a sign that you love the skin your in. If you find it easy and habitual to speak ill of someone else, this is indicative of you NOT loving the skin your in.

It takes guts to be okay with yourself, and publicly display it with grace and humility. The changing seasons can't dictate how you will display self affection. Just because you don't get the job, or you don't know how things are going to pan out doesn't mean that you become self injurious. Love the skin your in. Practice it. Live it, be it, and thank God that you have a voice.

When you really start to love the skin that you are in, you won't let others mark you up or pick your old wounds. You will be watchful, but more focused on what you are putting in your ears and eye gate, than what people are saying. You have the power to stay and listen to what people would negatively say or simply walk away.

You have to get to a point that when you hear or see things that are contrary to what you know, it does not affect you. You have to get to the place where you are too sure of what God is, did, and wants to do, so that you are pressing toward the prize of the high calling which is in Christ Jesus.

Love the skin your in, praise God for the all the additional things coming your way.

Chapter Fourteen
The Journey is the Risk and the Reward
"Obstacles Are Things That Are Seen When You Take Your Eyes Off Your Goals"

As we come to the close of this particular chapter of my life, and possibly yours, I had to sit and ponder about the journey. The good, the bad, and truly the ugly and through it all, I saw GRACE and experienced VICTORY.

I saw that the journey itself was a risk, but it also became my reward. I say this because while, I did not have any financial guarantees, my hope was solidly built on what I knew about God, and His word, and this is what fostered the reward.

The word *journey* means traveling from one place to another, usually taking a rather long time or trip. It is a distance, course, or area traveled or that is suitable for traveling. A *journey* is a passage or progress from one stage to another: the journey to success.

So my journey was the traveling of being in stagnation, frustration and a very bad mental state, while I deal with two young children, no job, the spoils of a bad marriage, abuse, and the shame of settling in the first place. To go distance, and actually come out, is the reward.

As I made declarations and decrees of God's word over my life and continue to make the decision to confess my possibility versus my limitations and lack, I could only see reward in my future.

When I felt even the glimmer of hope, I held on to it, until it grew bigger, and I was able to cast off that area of doubt, and move closer to fully believing God's word for me. It was during this time that I had to break it down to its simplest form, and look at the entire plan of God, as it was written in scripture, and fortunate for me, I saw that He included me in the world of hope and change and that by itself was a reward.

Yes your journey will be risky, even probably scary but I am telling you except you make the decision to do something you have never done, you won't have the things that you want to have. Your reward is in finishing the race that has your name on it. You must cross that finish line.

There is a world of specific people in certain areas, waiting to hear the RESOLVE of your story, not just the process. They want to see the demonstration of your plan, your deliverance, and what you do with it all.

So what will you do with your pain and suffering, your trials and tribulations, your success and failures? Will you use your experiences to fuel your emotional pity party, or will you take a stand, and use it to be a light to those who are in constant darkness.

I know that during my journey, I physically did not have the right tools at the time, including money, sometimes lights, water, car, but somehow, God gave me the strength, to keep my eye on the reward.

You will have many opportunities to enjoy the process but only one opportunity to give your account of victory, and that is when you have gone to the other side. When you have appreciated the safety and covering during the ride of what you know is God's hand, you will you know the value of the end of this journey is much more than what you might lose along the way.

Unfortunately I am sure there will be many more things that you will endure in this life, but at least now you will the perspective to think a different way, and not rely on old patterns of experiences to guide you into a new truth and shifted perspective.

I find that now that I am on the Loving It side, I even laugh at the many temper tantrums I had about this not happening and that not working, so to the point where, I am almost ashamed of myself for carrying on in such a manner. But it happens.

I made it thus far, and I will believe God to take me further, that if He began a good work in me, he will complete it also. The same is true for you. Believe the Word of God against all odds, you were made to defy IMPOSSIBILITIES, so live up to your creation.

BONUS Chapters and Writings: To Inspire and Encourage

Now that you have read the book and gotten snippets of my 5 year journey of finding me, and loving me anew, I wanted to add some writings, and articles that have blessed me along the way, that I am sure will bless you.

It is my utmost desire to leave an expression of hope and inspiration in your life, that speaks volumes to where you are going. I pray that every step you take it is ordered by the Lord, and you know it, and recognize it.

Take heart today and be encouraged, that you Starting Over, is not in vain, but it is a natural progression of growth, and a deliberate attempt to be all that God has called you to be. Enjoy and may the King of Glory shine his light on you.

Chapter Fifteen

The Best Way to Help Others

There are many ways to help people in our society. You can give them money, food, shelter, clothe or some other tangible thing. I have learned throughout my life that one of the best things that I can do to help others is to **educate, empower and equip** them for successful living.

I do this by motivating, inspiring, training and teaching them how to change the way they see their life. This is my life mission, and I do this by using Biblical principles, psychosocial interventions, and any other thing that will positively get the desired result.

As a child I grew up in rather harsh but interesting conditions, where drugs, alcohol, and familial dysfunction plagued me and tried to severely disrupt my entire life, and cause me to abort the life that I was destined to have; but because I was taught early on that, there was a purpose for my life, somehow I weathered through the storms.

The life that I had and lived was not easy, but early on many adults fostered an environment that educated, empowered and equipped me to be successful in what I did; essentially in who I am now.

As we continue throughout this year, we must remember what's important, and put first things first. Now, what's important to me may not be important to you, but I just want to leave you with a thought.

Life's importance should not be focused on how much money you or I make, or how big our house is, or what kind of car we drive but it should be focused on who I help and how I empower them to make positive changes in their life.

The way you help others is totally your decision, but for me, I have decided to let my life and its experiences create an atmosphere of change, growth and transformation, so that people can reach their maximum potential and create the cycle all over again in someone else.

As you consider what things you should continue to do this year, keep this in mind: There are always some things that we can cut off that would allow us to grow faster. It is never the rule, but always the exception, that we were created to be a blessing,

Change Your Life Reflection Moment:
1. **How do you help people?**
2. **Does helping others cause you to forget about what you are going through?**
3. **Should you forget about what you are going through?**

Chapter Sixteen

When Life Gets Clogged UP The Desire For ORder
June 6, 2010

One day my niece Ladaysha put on her facebook profile asking the question "am I the only person who feels like if their room/area/house isn't together and organized then certain parts of their life are also unorganized and nothing goes as smoothly as it could.?" Then she proceeded to say, "sounds crazy but that's just how my brain operates, but now that my room is clean/organized again I feel better."

When I read this information, I begin to think about my own life, and how at times, it can get disorderly, chaotic, and down right unmanageable. Then I started thinking more globally with people, women in general and decided to respond back to her, and it started a discussion that makes me to know that we all desire order in our lives, but sometimes life just gets clogged up.

For those of you who commute, have children, a demanding life that seems to have wheels that won't stop, then I am hoping that this article speaks to you. I realized, and as I encouraged me niece to know that with disorder, comes chaos, and simplicity is out the window.

It is my belief and my experience that order creates simplicity, which in my opinion is why most people even me at times, are working too hard to accomplish things. The culprit: DISORDER. This leaves us feeling overworked, not fulfilled, always feeling shut down, tired, overwhelmed, fatigued, and always distracted.

This distraction is the very thing that starts the clog up that takes place in our life. We turn our heads away from what we are doing and something else gets in that space, and now we are 1 thing away from completing our targeted thing. Then we move on in life, and allow another distraction.

So now there are two things in our way of our desired goal. Before we know we are 5 distractions deep and our life is clogged up with stuff. Here are some things that you can think about when you need to unclog your day:

1. Identify your true purpose for the day (complete all task at work, or clean your house)

2. Put a time frame on the task (3 hours (9am-12pm)

3. Don't stop the task until the time frame is up.

4. Try not to multi-task things that you have identified as important, just complete the task first, leaving no room for procrastination

5. Make yourself a priority, and do steps 1 through 4 all over again with you in mind.

Just like you would use drano to fix your sink or call a plumber to unclog your toilet, you need something to unclog your life, and the greatest thing that I can think of is time, and priority.

The next time you have girltalk, with your friends or man time with your buddies, ask them have they unclogged their life, and then share with them how to do it. It works, because I am doing it right now.

Inspiring Thought: *Your ability to see past your own errors, is the beginning of your sight being fully on God and not on you.*

Change Your Life Reflection Moment

1. What in your life is out of order?
2. What is being clogged up?
3. Who haven't you forgiven? Did you include yourself?
4. What needs to be thrown away today, right now?

Chapter Seventeen

Upgrade Your Worth

Upgrade Your Worth: (Step 1)

While you may think that you know your worth even the greatest of us forgets every now and then what we really are worth, and why? In my season of "many projects", I am having to do a lot *rethinking, reassessing, reformatting, and re-branding* everything about me and that which is very dear to me!

If you are ready to upgrade your worth, you must first quit talking about what you don't have and focus on what you do have. Too often you speak the current truth of your situation as a permanent fact, and you get stuck there and your words ensnare you.

Scripture is rather emphatic about watching our words and how it brings either life or death! So confess not what is "true" but what is the "truth" about your life and it's worth.

Take the following steps:

1. Write down every job title, church title what you did, how much you made and the impact that you made there.

2. If you remember one significant thing that you learned from each of the experiences you had, write it down.

3. Ask yourself has my life been enriched by the experiences that I have had in my past? Have I learned from them? Am I further along then when I started? Whose fault is that?

4. Has someone else's life been increased, enriched because of what you have walked through?

5. Write down how much you think you are worth, and don't simply base it in financial terms. Do it in terms of your time, respect etc.

Upgrade Your Worth is an excerpt of the individual and group coaching/training program of Speak With A Purpose

I felt that I knew exactly what my worth was and value, but I only referred to it in terms of dollars and cents, and not in the fullness of who I was, and what God had made me be.

Your life's experiences, have caused your worth and value to increase especially if you have been fortunate to share the story with others. Their lives become enriched, in which they can withdraw information from, dodging many bullets, and living a life fully on purpose.

You will only respect and honor what you want, and so will others. If they really want to be around you, purchase products from you, then they will honor your time and your prices, and will not try and talk you down.

When people do ask you for more time than is allotted or that you can do, there is something you are giving off, that suggest to them that you would lower your original statement about time and space.

Your value, your worth, is only upgraded, when you realize that it is time.

Chapter Eighteen

The Peace Within
"A Chat To Women"

When women build healthy relationships, there is a beautiful thing that happens with connection, energy and spirit. For this to remain true, each woman must be willing to have and demonstrate peace from within.

This peace is not focused on how nice or kind you speak things to others, but rather, how clear and to what intent you live things from the inside out.

As women we have many roles, jobs, and opportunities that sometimes distract us from the purpose of being a friend, mother, lover, or president of a company. Yet, the common thread that holds us all together is the power of having peace within your very being.

Peace is something I know that I crave for, but found out that I can't have it on my own. I know what makes me unpeaceful and what changes my internal status, but the kind of peace that gives you the knowing that "all things have already worked out", comes from God.

I learned very early on in my Christian walk that there were some things I was just going to have to always have, and that was God's peace, presence, and spirit of prayer.

The spirit of peace calms you when you are in the tempest of your storm, and frees you when you feel bound by everything else. Peace is the weapon that chases confusion out, and gives serenity when there is no evidence that there should be. Peace becomes a comfort place, and a desired place, especially when you seek for the author of peace.

To have Christ, is to have peace within. Won't you keep Him near?

Chapter Nineteen

THE PURPOSE AND PURSUIT OF FOCUS
The Book of Nehemiah
(Chapter 1-4)
HISTORICAL BACKGROUND

In the Hebrew manuscripts Ezra and Nehemiah appeared as one book. It is not certain who the author is but is given to Nehemiah for the most part. Nehemiah was a governor at the time, but the story also indicates that he was a cup bearer for the King. The book continues from 2 Chronicles.

As a Jewish official, who was appointed governor in Judea with the responsibility of rebuilding of Jerusalem, the book of Nehemiah acts as a narrative of the restoration of the Jewish people to its homeland. The decrees of two Persian Kings, Cyrus and Artaxerxes, and restoration seem as a part of their demand.

Nehemiah completed his task, and remained governor for 12 years and enlarged the city's population by resettling villagers in the Capital. Nehemiah then returned and carried out a second term and carried out reforms of the religious life and community of Jerusalem (the rehearsal of certain divine laws and the restoration of ancient ordinances.

The rebuilding of the walls of Jerusalem consider as a type of the up-building of the divine kingdom in the earth. Just as Nehemiah had to build what was now a wasteland so must you rebuild your house (life), and put the necessary things in place to fortify you against the next ambush.

We will all have attacks, and sometimes flat out wars, but take heart and know that God is for you and He will be with you.

KEY DEFINITIONS FOR THIS STUDY:

PURSUIT:
1. The act of pursuing
2. An effort to secure or attain; quest
3. Any occupation, pastime, or the like in which a person is engaged regularly or customarily

SYNONYMS: CHASE, HUNT, SEARCH, INCLINATION, ACTIVITY, PREOCCUPATION

PURPOSE:
1. The reason for which something exists or is done, made, used
2. An intended or desired result; end; aim; goal
3. Determination; resoluteness
4. The subject in hand; the point at issue
5. Practical result, effect, or advantage:
6. To set as an aim, intention, or goal for oneself
7. To intend; origin
8. To resolve to do something

WRATH:
1. Strong, stern or fierce anger
2. Deeply resentful indignation
3. Vengeance or punishment as the consequence of anger

CONTEMPT:
1. The feeling with which a person regards anything considered mean, vile, or worthless; disdain; scorn
2. The state of being despised; dishonor; disgrace
3. Willful disobedience to or open disrespect for the rules or orders of a court
4. An act showing such disrespect

QUICK FACTS ABOUT THE BOOK OF NEHEMIAH

1. The Walls broken down (waste, rubble)

2. The preliminary season of fasting and prayer may typify the stat of mind which should proceed all great spiritual enterprises

3. Nehemiah's sacrifice of a fine position for the good of the cause may typify the sacrificial service always needed when a great work is to be accomplished

4. The night inspection of the city, may typify the necessity of facing the facts before beginning constructive work.

5. The seeking of cooperation may typify an essential element in all work.

6. The enlistment of all classes may typify the importance of through organization

WHAT YOU MAY HAVE TO ENDURE WHEN YOU START TO BUILD

1. **Ridicule-** overcome by confidence in God

2. **Wrath and Contempt-** overcome by prayer and hard work

3. **Conspiracy-** overcome by watchfulness and prayer

4. **Discouragement of friends-** overcome by steadfast courage

5. **Selfish Greed-** overcome by rebuke and self-sacrificing

The **RESULT-** work completed, enemy confounded by persistent endeavor

QUICK INFORMATION FROM CHAPTER 1-4

CHAPTER 1:

- Nehemiah Is Informed That His City Is In Complete Ruins

- Nehemiah Mourns For The Loss

- Nehemiah Prays For Himself, For Help From God

- Nehemiah Prays For His People Because It Seems As If No one Cares About The State Of The City

- Nehemiah Becomes Emotionally Attached To The Process

CHAPTER 2:

- It Is Told To Us That Nehemiah Is The Kings Cupbearer, Drinking The Wine Before The King Indicating Risk, Loyalty And A Sense Of Commitment To The Leadership Within The Province Of Jerusalem

- The People Around You Will Notice A Need For You

- To Be About God's Present Business And Will Assist

- You Should Know The Time Of The Journey

- You Should Know What's Needed For The Journey

- You Should Understand The Mission Of The Job, And When You Do, People Will Follow You

- At The Time That They Gather Themselves, Their Enemies Appear On The Scene To Announce Themselves\

- Nehemiah Demonstrates His Confidence In God

CHAPTER 3:

Indicates the names and the order of those who helped build certain gates. This was to show the different classes of people involved in the rebuild process of Jerusalem.

CHAPTER 4:

- When Sanballat Heard Nehemiah And Them Had Built The Wall They Were Filled With Wroth, Indignation And Mocked The Jews

- The Enemy Will Always Try To Use Threatening Words To Discourage And Discredit You When You Are Building

- The Builders Withstood The Pressure Because They Had A Mind To Work

- Sanballat And Tobiah Heard It, They Said Let's Fight Them To Get Them To Quit Working

- They Made Their Prayer (Vow) To God And Stayed On The Wall, Working And Watching

20 Things To Know About
PURPOSE AND PURSUIT OF FOCUS
(FROM NEHEMIAH CHAPTERS 1-4)

1. **THERE WILL ALWAYS BE A NEED** *(The Why Of What's Going On)*

2. **SOMEONE WILL ALWAYS HAVE COMPASSION** *(To Do Something About The Need As God Will Always Have A Witness)*

3. **A TIME OF PERSONAL PRAYER** *(Where Instructions Are Sought So As To Know What To Do*

4. **A TIME OF PERSONAL BROKENESS** *(Where Nehemiah Found Himself Sad Because Of The Conditions)*

5. **A TIME TO REVEAL THE SOURCE OF YOUR BROKENESS** *(Nehemiah 2:3)*

6. **A TIME OF BELIEF** *(Having A Sense Of Patriotism, Loyalty)*

7. **A TIME OF READINESS** *(Nehemiah 2:5) (Knowing What To Do With What's Going On)*

8. **BE PREPARED FOR THE OPPOSITION WHO WILL BE MAD JUST AT KNOWING THAT YOU WANT DO SOMETHING** *(Nehemiah 2:15) (A Time of Mental Preparation)*

9. **YOU MUST TAKE THE FEW THAT GOD HAS GIVEN YOU AND SURVEY THE LAND/PROJECT** *(Do Your Due Diligence Before)*

10. **TIME TO EXPLAIN THE VISION AND THE EVENTS** *(Nehemiah 2:17-18) (You Must Know What The Vision Is and Explain It)*

11. **BECAUSE OF THE VISION, INSIGHT AND LEADERSHIP OF NEHEMIAH HE SAID LETS RISE UP AND BUILD AND THE PEOPLE FOLLOWED.** *(People Will Always Follow A Leader Models What They Are Saying And Who Truly Has A Vision)*

12. **SANBALLAT AND TOBIAH LAUGHED AND SCORN, BECAUSE THEY SAID THAT NEHEMIAH WAS REBELLING AGAINST THE KING** *(But They Did It To Discourage and Distract Them)*

13. **CAUSE YOU TO HAVE CONFIDENCE IN GOD**

14. **WILL ALWAYS CREAT ENEMIES AND THEY WILL HAVE WRATH, INDIGNATION AND MOCK YOU OF YOUR DEALINGS**

15. **THEY WILL TRY AND DISCOURAGE YOU BY THE WORDS THEY SAY**

16. **BUT YOU MUST REMAIN FOCUSED WITH THE TASK AT HAND**

17. **REMIND THE PEOPLE OF WHAT GOD HAS SAID AND WHO HE IS** *(Nehemiah 4:14) (People Respect God's Word and Truth)*

18. **ENEMIES WILL COME, BUT THEY WILL SEE YOU READY** *(Be Ready)*

19. **PRAY, WATCH, BUILD AND FIGHT IS THE KEY**

20. **THEY WERE NOT CONCERNED ABOUT HOW THEY LOOKED, THEY JUST GOT THE JOB DONE AND NEVER STOPPED EXCEPT TO WASH THEMSELVES.** *(You Can Not Quit)*

About the Author

Lakita D. Long is the Founder and Director of Inspiring You Ministries, Inc. a non-profit public charity organization that has helped mobilize more than 5,000 people into various forms of social, civic and spiritual involvement, resulting in powerful change in the community. She is also the creator of Change Your Life Seminars, Girltalk Program and Conferences, Host of Thinking Outloud Radio Show, and the Inspiring Voice behind God Is The Business Marketplace Ministry.

She is the author of When Believers Becomes Depressed: Helping Those Who Believe in God, God Is The Business...And He Wants Everyone Employed, Co-Author and Publisher of Change Your Life: The 90 Day Experience, and the Co-Author and Publisher of Change Your Life: Perfecting Your Purpose.

Known as a Speaker of Women's Conferences and Business Organizations, she is trained as a therapist often dubbed as "the people's therapist", provides Christian Counseling, is an Evangelist, and has committed her life to motivating, inspiring training, teaching and transferring information to all who will hear.

She holds several degrees in Psychology, Counseling, and Social Psychology, but credits all she knows through the many years of experience, and grace that was given to her by God.

She resides in Antioch, California with her two children Cayla and Jailen, and is glad to be their mom

For speaking engagements Lakita D. Long can be reached:

Email: drlakitagirltalk@aol.com
Facebook: Facebook.com/LakitaDeniseLong
Website: www.Godisthebusiness.com
Phone: 925-238-8711

www.ingramcontent.com/pod-product-compliance
Lightning Source LLC
Chambersburg PA
CBHW060810050426
42449CB00008B/1619